A CONRAD COMPANION

A CONRAD COMPANION

NORMAN PAGE

St. Martin's Press   New York

© Norman Page 1986

All rights reserved. For information, write:
St. Martin's Press, Inc.
175 Fifth Avenue, New York, NY 10010
Printed in Hong Kong
Published in the United Kingdom by
The Macmillan Press Ltd.
First published in the United States of America in 1986

ISBN 0–312–16261–8

Library of Congress Cataloging in Publication Data
Page, Norman.
A Conrad companion.
"Filmography": p.
Bibliography: p.
Includes index.
1. Conrad, Joseph, 1857–1924. 2. Novelists,
English—20th century—Biography. I. Title.
PR6005.04Z78478 1985   823'.912   85–11998
ISBN 0–312–16261–8

To Barnaby

Contents

List of Plates and Maps

Maps 1 and 3 are reproduced from Karl and Davies (eds), *The Collected Letters of Joseph Conrad*, vol. 1, by courtesy of the Cambridge University Press. Map 2 is reproduced from N. Sherry, *Conrad's Western World*, by courtesy of the Cambridge University Press.

Acknowledgements

The author and publishers wish to thank the following who have kindly given permission for the use of copyright material: The Mansell Collection, for plates 1, 3, 8, 9 and 12; The Beinecke Rare Book and Manuscript Library, Yale University, for plates 2 and 5; The National Library of Warsaw, for plate 4; the Estate of John Conrad, for plates 6 (photography by William Cadby) and 7 (photograph by T. and R. Annan and Sons); Sir Rupert Hart-Davis/Mrs Eva Reichmann, for plate 10; Richard Garnett, for plate 11; University of Texas Library, for plate 13; Duke University Library, North Carolina (the Virginia Grey Fund), for plate 14; The National Maritime Museum, for plate 15; and Norman Sherry, for plate 16.

Every effort has been made to trace all the copyright holders but if any have been inadvertently overlooked, the publishers will be pleased to make the necessary arrangement at the first opportunity.

Preface

The case of Joseph Conrad has many unusual features, and there are some aspects that may fairly be described as unique. Most obviously, he is, as M. C. Bradbrook put it long ago, 'Poland's English genius': other authors such as Nabokov and Beckett have written extensively in a language other than their native tongue, but Conrad is remarkable both for having written *only* in English and for having begun to learn English, which was not even his second language, at a relatively advanced age. Eventually he settled in England; adopted – or, according to his own account, was adopted by – the English language; married an English-woman; fathered sons who were brought up as English boys; and had a circle of friends who were largely English or English-speaking. Yet, as some of the evidence cited in the sections below titled 'Conrad Observed' and 'Conrad's Languages' suggests, he remained to the end of his life very much the foreigner in speech and manners; and this is an important factor in arriving at an understanding of his temperament and outlook. Like his contemporaries Henry James and Rudyard Kipling, he was both an insider and an outsider in relation to the English scene. His short story 'Amy Foster' is a moving allegory of his own experience, and when he fell ill Conrad, like Janko in that story (whose name is a near-anagram of 'J. Konrad'), reverted to Polish in his delirium.

But becoming an author was for Conrad a new start at a time when most men have long made their choices for life. In his thirty-eighth year when his first book appeared, he had behind him a career – not unsuccessful, though less successful than he sometimes liked to imply – as a merchant seaman. Work, duty, responsibility, solidarity: these and other key-concepts of Conrad's moral world as expressed in his fiction have nothing abstract or academic about them but are drawn from nearly twenty years at sea. Yet Conrad, it is clear, was far from being a typical mariner: apart from anything else, his origins in the Polish *szlachta* or ruling class, partly manifested in an aristocratic courtliness of manner and a punctiliousness over dress and personal appearance, marked him off from his fellows. When he turned to writing, it was inevitable that he should draw on his memories of ships and sailors; and indeed, having little else to draw on, he had little choice. For his experience, so rich in some areas, had been remarkably limited in others. He knew the oceans, the life of sailors, sailing and steam vessels, and many of the world's ports; but of life ashore, of occupations other than seafaring, of social or family life, and of the female half of the human race, his knowledge was severely restricted, and his early writings – welcomed by contemporaries as opening up new fictional territory – are also notable for what they leave out or avoid.

Understandably, Conrad himself sometimes became exasperated when reviewers and readers showed signs of typecasting him as a writer of sea-stories and purveyor of exotic backgrounds: a sort of latter-day blend of Captain Marryat and Robert Louis Stevenson, or of Pierre Loti and Rudyard Kipling. As he told a correspondent in 1906, 'They want to banish me to the middle of the ocean'; and later, when a collected edition of his works was being prepared, he insisted that 'all reference to the sea' should be avoided and made it clear that he did not wish to be offered to the public as 'a writer of the sea – or even of the tropics'. In 1917 he told Sidney Colvin:

> Perhaps you won't find it presumptuous if, after 22 years of work, I may say that I have not been very well understood. I have been called a writer of the sea, of the tropics, a descriptive writer, a romantic writer – and also a realist. But as a matter of fact all my concern has been with the 'ideal' value of things, events and people. That and nothing else . . .

Near the end of his life he told Richard Curle that 'in the body of my work barely one-tenth is what may be called sea stuff'. The tendency to regard him as primarily a writer of 'sea stuff' is not altogether a thing of the past; and it is important to remember that, for Conrad, the *Narcissus* (for all the precision and authenticity of detail with which it is evoked) is a microcosm of the larger world; that Jim's leap from the *Patna* is a type of human action; and that the sailor's life is only a special case of universal experience, though it is true that certain qualities such as isolation and solidarity may be more acutely and dramatically manifested at sea than ashore.

The pattern of Conrad's career as a writer, and the history of his reputation, are other curious features. Although his early work was praised by many reviewers, it did not sell; and the story of Conrad's chronic financial troubles and of the meagre rewards for creative efforts that at times drove him to a state of physical and mental collapse makes distressing reading. With *Chance* (1913) came success; but many of his critics have taken the view that by then, with only one or two exceptions, his period as a major artist was over. The 'achievement and decline' view of Conrad's career is persuasive, and certainly one would be reluctant to exchange a single page of *Lord Jim* or *The Secret Agent* for the whole of a book such as *The Arrow of Gold*. Conrad wrote to his American publisher Doubleday in 1918:

> I am sufficient of a democrat to detest the idea of being a writer of any 'coterie' of some small self-appointed aristocracy in the vast domain of art or letters. As a matter of feeling – not as a matter of business – I want to be read by many eyes and by all kinds of them, at last . . .

It is an irony of Conradian bitterness and intensity that he could, in his lifetime, reach 'many eyes and . . . all kinds of them' only after his work had sunk to a level little above that of mediocrity.

In the sixty years since Conrad's death, however, justice has been done to the earlier and finer work, and he is now acknowledged as one of the major figures of modernism and as one who, even before the nineteenth century ended, was hard at work remaking the novel and (in, for instance, *The Nigger of the 'Narcissus'* and *Heart of Darkness*) extending the possibilities of fiction. He is in our time one of the most widely studied and intensively discussed of modern authors, and in recent years there have been several contributions to Conrad scholarship and criticism that have significantly added to our knowledge and modified our understanding of his life, personality and writings. I refer to such works as the first instalment of Ian Watt's long-meditated and long-awaited critical and biographical study

Conrad in the Nineteenth Century (1980), the first volume of the
collected edition of Conrad's letters (*The Collected Letters of Joseph
Conrad, Volume 1, 1861–1897*, ed. Frederick R. Karl & Laurence
Davies (1983)), and what must now be regarded as the definitive
biography, Zdzislaw Najder's *Joseph Conrad: a Chronicle* (1983),
hereafter referred to, frequently and gratefully, as 'Najder'.

It has long been known that Conrad was an unreliable guide to
his own past history, but Najder's exhaustively researched and
fully documented study makes clear, as never before, the extraordinary extent of his lapses of memory, his self-deceptions, and
what in some instances can only be regarded as his lies. Again and
again, Najder sets the record straight. The autobiographical *A
Personal Record*, which Conrad described as 'absolutely genuine',
recounts his three examinations in order to qualify first as a ship's
officer and then as a master, but says nothing of the failures that
were also part of his record. 'Haven't I commanded an Australian
ship for over two years?' boasted Conrad in 1912. Certainly not,
retorts Najder: the command was of 'a small barque with a crew of
nine' and lasted for fourteen months. Recalling his childhood in
Poland, he states that he spent the last eighteen months of his
father's life with him in Cracow; actually the period was four
months. Najder's chronicle is shot through with similar examples.
We now know – what many had long suspected – that Conrad
passed off as a duelling wound what was actually the result of a
suicide attempt; that he invented the story of an accident suffered
on board the *Annie Frost* (on which he never served); and that
whereas he claimed that Edward Garnett had urged him to begin
a second novel, *An Outcast of the Islands* had been begun before his
meeting with Garnett. All this means that great caution is
necessary in dealing with Conrad's statements: he is notoriously
unreliable about dates (to put it as charitably as possible), and
even gets his son's birthday wrong.

But it is not only in relation to Conrad's biography that these
errors or deceptions are significant. For they represent part of a
self-mythologizing process that proceeded from the desire to
rewrite the story of his own life in more dramatic and heroic terms
than reality justified. This tendency seems to have become second
nature and was no doubt, in part at least, unconscious; and since
the autobiographical element looms so large in the novels and
stories, the process played an important role in the genesis and
composition of his fiction. The whole question of the relationship

between memory and invention, history and fiction, in Conrad's work is a more complex one than has sometimes been supposed; and we need to take with a good pinch of salt his rather insistent and unqualified claims for the authenticity of his material – when, for example, he describes 'Youth' as 'a feat of memory' and 'a record of experience', or *The Shadow-Line* as 'exact autobiography'.

Many of Conrad's embellishments of the truth were intended, consciously or otherwise, to transform the random and accidental happenings that make up a life into purposeful, meaningful, long-premeditated events: to turn a chronicle into a plot. Thus his becoming a British seaman is depicted by Conrad as the product of the slow workings of destiny, whereas it appears to have been largely a matter of chance. But all this would be of only minor psychological interest were it not that the activity extended into his creative life. As Najder points out, there is a continuity between the fictions of Conrad's life and the life of his fictions: 'The legend was an attempt to make his life meaningful. But Conrad's works as a whole . . . represent an attempt to find the meaning of human existence in general' (p. 494). In his recent *Dickens and Women* (1983), Michael Slater has described Dickens as 'a supreme dramatizer of his own past, adept at organizing its incidents into a coherent plot' (p. 113), and much the same can be said of Conrad – as it can, no doubt, of many other writers as well as of many of us who are not major novelists. As Frederick Crews pointed out in a review of Najder's biography in the *New York Review of Books* (1 March 1984), much of Conrad's fiction is, avowedly or otherwise, more or less autobiographical; but not only the fiction but also the non-fictional writings and the letters – and even the accounts of such members of Conrad's circle as Jessie Conrad and Ford Madox Ford – need to be approached very circumspectly. What Najder has achieved, very strikingly, is the 'demythification' of Conrad, replacing the self-dramatizing legend by objective biography based wherever possible on documentary evidence.

All this adds up to a man and a writer full of fascination but also full of pitfalls for the unwary who approach the problems with uncritical reverence rather than sympathetic scepticism. The present volume attempts to provide a guide to Conrad's life, background and writings that embodies some of the findings of recent scholarship. It is intended both for the student who wishes to acquaint himself with the outline of Conrad's career and to gain an overview of his work, and also for the reader who knows his Conrad but will often need to check a date, name or fact, and should find that the information he seeks lies more conveniently to hand than in critical or biographical studies not primarily organized as works of reference. The biographical sections – 'A Conrad Chronology', 'A Conrad Who's Who', 'Conrad's World', 'Conrad Observed', and 'Conrad's Languages' – are followed by sections devoted to his fictional and non-fictional writings, wherein the student and reader will find information on the genesis, composition, publication and reception of Conrad's books together with an indication of some of the main lines of interpretation, criticism and evaluation.

Throughout (as, indeed, will be obvious) I have been greatly indebted to many of Conrad's biographers and critics, and especially to Jocelyn Baines, Albert Guerard, Douglas Hewitt, Zdzislaw Najder, Norman Sherry and Ian Watt, details of whose publications will be found in the Select Bibliography. I am grateful to Barnaby Page for compiling the filmography, and to Marguerite Meyers and her colleagues for help with typing.

The author and publishers wish to thank the Cambridge University Press for permission to use an extract from *John Conrad, Joseph Conrad: Times Remembered* (1981).

A Conrad Chronology

Further information concerning individuals and places referred to below will be found in the sections 'A Conrad Who's Who' and 'Conrad's World'. The chronology of Conrad's life is very problematical at many points, and different authorities sometimes give a variety of dates for the same event. The information below is based on the most recent research, but in some instances dates need to be regarded as tentative.

1857   (3 December) Józef Teodor Konrad Nalecz Korzeniowski* born at Berdyczów (Berdichev) in the Ukraine, first and only child of Apollo and Ewa Korzeniowski.

1859   The Korzeniowski family move to Zhitomir, where Apollo works in a publishing house.

1861   (May) They move to Warsaw, where Apollo has been invited to edit a new literary magazine. He is involved in political activities, and on 21 October is arrested and spends seven months in prison; his wife is also accused.

1862   (9 May) They are both sentenced to deportation, and leave under police escort for Vologda, about 300 miles north-east of Moscow. Józef develops pneumonia during the journey. In Vologda, Ewa, who is suffering from tuberculosis, falls seriously ill.

1863   From the age of five, Conrad is 'a great reader' (*A Personal*

---

* 'Jósef and Teodor were the given names of his paternal and maternal grandfathers respectively; but as a child he was called Konrad (or Konradek), and the associations of that name were wholly literary and patriotic. "For a Pole," Czeslaw Milosz writes, "the name Konrad symbolizes the anti-Russian fighter and resister." This is largely because of Adam Mickiewicz's long narrative poem, *Konrad Wallenrod* (1828)' (Ian Watt, *Conrad in the Nineteenth Century*, pp. 6–7).

Record). In January the family are permitted to move south to Chernikhov, near Kiev. In August Ewa takes her son on a three-month visit to Nowachwastów, where her brother Tadeusz Bobrowski has an estate. Her health now deteriorates rapidly.

1865   (18 April) Death of Ewa Korzeniowska from tuberculosis.

1866   (May) Conrad spends the summer with his uncle and grandmother in Nowachwastów and has his first sight of the sea (at Odessa). In October he returns to his father but falls ill and is taken by his grandmother to Kiev for treatment and then to his uncle's estate for the rest of the winter. Meanwhile, Apollo's health also deteriorates (he is suffering from tuberculosis).

1868   (January) Apollo, who is now seriously ill, is permitted to return to Poland, and he and his son settle in Lvov.

1869   (February) They move to Cracow. (23 May) Death of Apollo Korzeniowski. In his funeral procession, which is 'a great patriotic manifestation' (Watt), Józef walks behind the hearse.

'The five years that followed [i.e. 1869–74] constitute the period in Conrad's life about which the least is known' (Najder). For the next few years, the boy is brought up in Austrian-occupied Poland by Teofila Bobrowska, his maternal grandmother. He attends schools irregularly in Cracow and Lvov, and is also taught by private tutors. His uncle Tadeusz Bobrowski soon assumes responsibility as his guardian. By 1872 Conrad has conceived an ambition to go to sea.

1873   (May) He is sent to Switzerland with his tutor on account of chest trouble, and spends several months there.

1874   (13 October) He leaves Cracow for Marseilles, where he has some distant relatives, the Chodzko family. On 15 December he sails for St Pierre, Martinique, as a passenger on the *Mont Blanc*, arriving on 16 February 1875.

1875   (30 March) He leaves St Pierre on the *Mont Blanc*. (23 May) He arrives back in Marseilles. (25 June) He sets off again on the same ship for the same destination, this time as apprentice, arriving in Le Havre on 23 December and making his way by train to Marseilles via Paris.

1876   After six months in Marseilles, he (8 July) sails again for St

Pierre, this time on the *Saint-Antoine*, nominally as a steward, arriving in Martinique on 18 August. The ship then visits ports in Colombia and Venezuela, arriving back in St Pierre on 16 September; goes to the Virgin Islands later in the same month; on 12 October sets out with a cargo of coal for Port-au-Prince; and leaves St Pierre for Marseilles on 25 November.

1877 (15 February) Conrad arrives back in Marseilles. He is prevented by an anal abscess from sailing with the *Saint-Antoine* again on 31 March. During this year he considers the possibility of service in the British merchant navy. Later in the year he may have been involved in gun-running to Spain (see *The Mirror of the Sea*), though Najder (p. 47) regards this as 'highly questionable if not impossible'. He loses a considerable amount of money, part of his patrimony sent to him by his uncle.

1878 According to one account, he borrows a further sum, loses it in the Monte Carlo casino, returns to Marseilles, and shoots himself in the chest, though without serious harm being done. (In later life Conrad accounted for the scars by speaking of a duel; the evidence, however, suggests a self-inflicted wound.) A fictionalized account of his experience appears in *The Arrow of Gold*. Uncle Tadeusz arrives in Marseilles on 11 March and pays off Conrad's debts. On 24 April, a premium having been paid for him as an apprentice, Conrad sets sail on the *Mavis*, a British steamer bound for Malta and Constantinople. By his own account it is on this ship that he hears his first words of spoken English. 'This turned out to be as momentous a step as his leaving Poland; but it is evident that Conrad did not recognize it as such at the time . . . and it is clear . . . that he can have had little inkling that he would spend fifteen years or so sailing throughout the world as a British seaman and become a British master mariner during the course of his career' (Baines). On 10 June he arrives in Lowestoft and quits the *Mavis*, now setting foot on English soil for the first time; he knows no-one in England, and almost nothing of the language. He visits London and on 11 July finds employment as an ordinary seaman, making three trips on the *Skimmer of the Sea* between Lowestoft and Newcastle and picking up English from the crew. He

leaves the *Skimmer* on 23 August and returns to London,
where 'No explorer could have been more lonely' ('Poland
Revisited', *Notes on Life and Letters*). On 12 October he joins
the *Duke of Sutherland* at Gravesend; this is a full-rigged
wool clipper bound for Sydney, and he is employed as an
ordinary seaman at a shilling a month. (26 December) The
ship passes the Cape of Good Hope.

1879   (31 January) Conrad arrives in Sydney and spends five
months there, acting as ship's night-watchman. Having at
last obtained a cargo, the ship leaves for England on 6 July,
reaching London on 19 October. On 12 December, he
leaves London as a member of the crew of the *Europa*, a
steamship bound for Greece.

1880   (30 January) Conrad leaves the *Europa* on its return to
London. He lives in lodgings in Holloway (North London)
and studies for the examination to qualify himself as
second mate, presenting himself for the examination on 28
May. (*A Personal Record* gives a vivid account of the
occasion, which was successful.) On 21 August he sails
from Tilbury as third mate of the *Loch Etive*, a full-rigged
ship bound for Sydney, where it arrives on 24 November
(there are references to the outward and the homeward
voyages in *The Mirror of the Sea*).

1881   (11 January) The *Loch Etive* leaves Sydney, reaching
London on 24 April. Conrad later alleged that he joined
the *Annie Frost* in June, sailed with her from Deal to Le
Havre and back to London, and was slightly injured in a
collision during the return voyage. Although many biographers have accepted his account, Najder dismisses it as
an invention and argues that Conrad had concocted the
story of an accident, the loss of his luggage, and a short
period in hospital (all reported to his uncle in a letter of 10
August) as an excuse for having spent all his money (see
Najder, pp. 70–1). Baines had earlier treated it as a
fabrication designed to extract money from his uncle. For
an example of its being taken seriously, see Jerry Allen, *The
Sea Years of Joseph Conrad*, pp. 151–3. On 19 September
Conrad joins the *Palestine* at Tilbury as second mate; this is
an old ship that, after picking up a cargo of coal from
Newcastle, is due to sail for Bangkok. (The ill-starred
voyage is the basis for 'Youth'.) The *Palestine* leaves

London on 21 September, runs into gales in the North Sea, is rammed by a steamer at Newcastle, and is delayed there for three weeks. On 29 November it leaves Newcastle, meets more rough weather in the Channel, and is kept afloat only by constant pumping. At Falmouth (Cornwall) the crew leave the ship; extensive repairs take nearly nine months.

1882 (17 September) The *Palestine* sails for Bangkok.

1883 (11 March) Between Java and Sumatra the cargo of coal shows signs of spontaneous combustion and (14 March) catches fire. The crew take to the boats and reach land safely the next day. They are subsequently taken to Singapore, arriving there on 22 March, and await a court of inquiry, which in due course exonerates both master and crew. Conrad spends a month in Singapore, setting sail for London on a Spanish steamship in mid-April. He reaches Port Said on 13 May and London by the end of the month. In late July he visits his uncle Tadeusz in Marienbad; and on 12 August they go together to Teplice for two weeks. On his return Conrad joins (10 September) the sailing ship *Riversdale* as second mate, bound for the Far East and Australasia. The ship sails from London on 13 September, spends two months at Port Elizabeth in South Africa, and reaches Madras on 8 April 1884. Meanwhile, Conrad has quarrelled with the captain, is relieved of his position, and

1884 (17 April) leaves the ship at Madras. After travelling to Bombay by rail, he signs on the homeward-bound *Narcissus* as second mate under Captain Duncan. The ship leaves Bombay on 3 June and reaches Dunkirk on 16 October – a voyage that is to provide the material for *The Nigger of the 'Narcissus'*. During the voyage, Joseph Barron, able seaman and apparently an American negro, dies at sea (24 September). Conrad spends the winter in London and on 3 December passes the examination to qualify as first mate, having failed at the first attempt on 17 November (the failure is unmentioned in his account of the examination in *A Personal Record*).

1885 (24 April) Conrad signs on under Captain Blake as second mate of the *Tilkhurst*, a sailing ship bound for the Far East. She sails from Hull to Cardiff and, after a delay of almost a month, sets out on 10 June for Singapore, arriving there on 22 September. After about a month there, she sails for Calcutta, arriving on 21 November; she spends seven weeks in that port.

1886 The *Tilkhurst* leaves Calcutta on 8 January and reaches Dundee on 17 June. (28 July) Conrad sits unsuccessfully the examination for his master's certificate. (18 August) He becomes a British citizen, and (10 November) obtains his master's certificate (see *A Personal Record*). (28 December) He signs on as second mate of the *Falconhurst*, sailing with it from London to Penarth and signing off on 2 January.

1887 (16 February) Conrad joins the *Highland Forest* in Amsterdam as first mate under Captain John McWhir; and, after some delay (described in *The Mirror of the Sea*) on account of cold weather, sets sail for Java. During the voyage he receives a back injury, and on reaching Samarang (Java) on 20 June is ordered by a doctor to leave the ship. He is taken to Singapore, spends six weeks in the European Hospital, and then enters the Officers' Sailors' Home for convalescence. He meets James Craig, captain of the steamer *Vidar*, and (22 August) joins that ship, making four trips to Borneo and acquiring thereby material that will be used in his first two novels.

1888 (4 January) Conrad leaves the *Vidar* and after a fortnight at the Sailors' Home in Singapore goes to Bangkok to take over as captain of the *Otago* (the ship had come from Adelaide and its captain had died at sea) – an experience that provided material for several stories, including 'The Secret Sharer' and *The Shadow-Line*. (24 January) He assumes his first command. (9 February) The *Otago* leaves Bangkok. (2 March) The *Otago* reaches Singapore, the *Singapore Free Press* reporting that 'the Captain wished to get a further supply of medicine before he proceeded on his journey' since 'several of the crew are suffering from fever'. (9 March) The *Otago* leaves Singapore for Sydney, arriving there on 7 May after weathering a gale. (22 May) The *Otago* leaves Sydney for Melbourne, returning on 12 July. (7 August) The *Otago* leaves Sydney for Mauritius via the Torres Strait, a notoriously hazardous route, arriving at

Port Louis on 30 September. (22 November) The *Otago* sets sail for Melbourne.

1889   (5 January) The *Otago* reaches Melbourne. After a month there, Conrad takes the ship to Minlaton (South Australia), arriving there on 22 February, and proceeds to Port Adelaide. He declines his employers' invitation to take it again to Mauritius; late in March he resigns his command, and (3 April) sails from Adelaide as a passenger on the steamship *Nurnberg*, reaching Southampton on 14 May and on his arrival in London taking rooms in Bessborough Gardens, Pimlico. On 31 March the Russian Ministry of Home Affairs releases him from the status of a Russian subject. One morning in September he 'sat down to write' (*A Personal Record*), this occasion apparently marking the beginning of work on *Almayer's Folly*. Meanwhile he works for a time as supercargo for a firm of shipowners. In November, he goes to Brussels for interview for the command of a Congo steamboat.

1890   (5 February) En route for the Ukraine, where he is to visit his uncle, he breaks his journey in Brussels and calls on his cousin, Alexsander Poradowski, who is seriously ill. He meets Alex's wife Marguerite. Poradowski dies on 7 February. Conrad spends two months on his uncle's estate. He is back in Brussels by the end of April and learns that, thanks to Marguerite Poradowska's influence, his three-year appointment in the Congo has been confirmed. On 10 May he sails from Bordeaux for the Congo on the *Ville de Maceio*, thus beginning 'the most traumatic journey of his life' (Najder). The ship calls at various ports, including Tenerife, Dakar, and Freetown, reaching Boma (about sixty miles up the Congo) on 12 June; he travels thence by steamer to Matadi, a further thirty miles up-river, where he meets Roger Casement; after two weeks there, he sets off (28 June) on a 230-mile trek overland to Kinshasa on Stanley Pool, arriving there on 1 August. There he finds that the steamer *Florida*, which he is supposed to command, has been badly damaged. (4 August) He sets off as supernumerary on the *Roi des Belges*, reaching Stanley Falls (about 1000 miles up-river) on 1 September. Conrad suffers from fever and dysentery, but is put in charge of the boat for the return journey after the captain is taken ill. (See also under entry for Klein in 'A Conrad Who's Who'.) (24 September) Conrad arrives back in Kinshasa after an eighteen-day journey. He learns that the command of the *Florida*, originally promised to him, has been given to another. (19 October) Suffering from dysentery and malaria, he travels downstream by canoe and at Boma embarks for England. (Almost nothing is known about Conrad's experiences in the closing months of 1890.)

1891   (January) Conrad, still suffering from malaria, arrives in Brussels (like Marlow in *Heart of Darkness*) and visits Marguerite Poradowska. He is in London by 1 February and spends about a month in hospital at Dalston, afflicted with physical and nervous disorders. At this period he probably takes rooms at 17 Gillingham Street, near Victoria Station. On 20 May he sets off for a spa near Geneva, leaving there on 14 June. On his way back to London he visits Marguerite again (she is now living in Paris). Attacks of malaria continue throughout the summer. (4 August) He takes a temporary job in a London warehouse and also works as a translator; then is offered the position of chief officer on the clipper *Torrens*, 'one of the most famous ships of her time' (Baines), which is bound for Australia under Captain W. H. Cope. He sets sail from Plymouth on 25 November.

1892   (28 February) The *Torrens* reaches Adelaide; after five weeks there, it sets sail (8 April) for England, arriving on 2 September. (25 October) Conrad sets out on a second voyage in the same ship to the same destination.

1893   (30 January) The *Torrens* arrives in Adelaide, leaving on 23 March. Among the passengers on the return journey are Edward Sanderson and John Galsworthy. On arriving in London (26 July), Conrad resigns his position on the *Torrens*. In August he goes to the Ukraine for about a month to visit his uncle. On returning to London, he is for a time unemployed. Work continues on *Almayer's Folly*. Towards the end of the year he meets his future wife, Jessie George (this according to one account by Jessie; in another she says 'early in November 1894'). On 29 November Conrad joins the *Adowa*, a British steamer; he sails from

London to Rouen and waits there for a month, working in the meantime at his novel (according to *A Personal Record*, ch. 10 was written in Rouen).

1894   Back in London, (17 January) Conrad leaves the *Adowa*, which has failed in its plan to convey French emigrants to Canada, and returns to 17 Gillingham Street. Work on *Almayer's Folly* continues: he is now less than three chapters from the end. In February he learns of the death of his uncle Tadeusz. In March he visits Marguerite in Brussels and in April stays with the Sanderson family in Elstree, Middlesex. (24 April) *Almayer's Folly* is completed after five years' intermittent work. At the beginning of May, Conrad receives the first part of his inheritance (about £120). Revisions to the novel are completed later in the month. (4 July) His novel is submitted to the publishing firm of Fisher Unwin and (October) accepted on the recommendation of their reader Edward Garnett; Conrad receives twenty pounds for the copyright. Then or soon afterwards Conrad meets Garnett, who (according to Conrad's later account) suggests that he write another novel, whereupon *An Outcast of the Islands* is begun. (Baines and Najder suggest, however, that the novel had been begun before the meeting with Garnett.)

1895   At the beginning of the year, Conrad writes the preface to *Almayer's Folly*. By about 1 February, he has written ten chapters of *An Outcast*. In March he spends a few days in Brussels. (29 April) *Almayer's Folly* is published under the name of Joseph Conrad; it receives favourable reviews but sells badly. On 2 May Conrad returns to the Swiss spa of Champel for a month and briefly courts a young French girl, Emilie Briquel. He continues work on *An Outcast*, completing it on 16 September. During this year he frequently meets and writes to Jessie George. In the autumn work begins on *The Sisters*.

1896   (February) Conrad proposes to Jessie George. (4 March) *An Outcast of the Island* is published. Conrad abandons *The Sisters* after writing about 10 000 words. (24 March) Conrad and Jessie George are married at a registry office in Hanover Square, London. The next day they set off for France, travelling via Southampton and St Malo, and spend nearly six months on the Brittany coast – first at the village of Lannion, then (from April) on Ile-Grande. There Conrad works on a novel that much later becomes *The Rescue* (temporarily abandoning it in August), and also writes three short stories: 'The Idiots' (published in *The Savoy* in October), 'The Lagoon' and 'An Outpost of Progress' (the last two are published in the following year). He also begins work on *The Nigger of the 'Narcissus'*. In late September the Conrads return to England and settle in a rented house in the village of Stanford-le-Hope, Essex, where work continues on 'my beloved Nigger'. They spend Christmas with a Polish family in Cardiff.

1897   (mid-January) Conrad completes *The Nigger of the 'Narcissus'*; revisions occupy another month, and later in the year he writes the Preface. The story is serialized in the *New Review* under W. E. Henley's editorship from August to December inclusive; it is published in New York (as *The Children of the Sea*) on 30 November and in England on 2 December. Early in the year Conrad writes 'Karain', which is published in *Blackwood's Magazine* in November. 'The Lagoon' appears in *Cornhill Magazine* in January and 'An Outpost of Progress' in *Cosmopolis* in June–July. In March the Conrads move to Ivy Walls, a farmhouse just outside Stanford-le-Hope. Conrad meets Henry James in February, Stephen Crane in October, and R. B. Cunninghame Graham in December. He writes 'The Return' (completed 24 September) and resumes work on *The Rescue*.

1898   (17 January) Birth of Borys Conrad. In February the Conrads spend two weeks with Stephen Crane at Oxted, Surrey. On 26 October the Conrads move to Pent Farm, near Aldington, Kent, rented from Ford Madox Hueffer, whom Conrad has recently met. *Tales of Unrest* is published on 4 April. Conrad writes 'Youth' (published in *Blackwood's Magazine* in September) and begins work (probably in April) on *Lord Jim* and (in mid-December) on *Heart of Darkness*. During this year he makes an unsuccessful attempt to get to sea again.

1899   (6 February) *Heart of Darkness* is finished; it is serialized in *Blackwood's Magazine* (February–April). In August Conrad becomes a client of J. B. Pinker, the literary agent. In

October serialization of *Lord Jim* begins in *Blackwood's*. Conrad collaborates with Hueffer on *The Inheritors*.

1900 In mid-March *The Inheritors* is finished. In April Marguerite Poradowska visits the Conrads. In May Conrad goes to Dover to see Stephen Crane for the last time (Crane dies on 5 June). (14 July) *Lord Jim* is finished, and (20 July) the Conrads join the Hueffers in Belgium for a month's holiday. (9 October) *Lord Jim* appears in volume form. In the last month of the year Conrad writes 'Typhoon' (finished January 1901).

1901 In May the Conrads spend two weeks with the Hueffers, who are now living at Winchelsea. Conrad finishes 'Falk' there and begins 'Amy Foster' (finished 18 June). *The Inheritors* is published on 26 June. For the rest of the year he works on *Romance*.

1902 'Tomorrow' is finished on 16 February and *Romance* in March. Conrad begins 'The End of the Tether', but on 23 June part of the manuscript is destroyed in a fire. (July) The Royal Literary Fund awards Conrad a grant of £300. (13 November) Publication of *Youth: A Narrative & Two Other Stories*. During this year Conrad takes up *The Rescue* again but soon puts it aside.

1903 *Nostromo* is begun. (22 April) Publication of *Typhoon, & Other Stories*. (16 October) *Romance* is published. During this year – 'a most disastrous year for my work' (letter of 26 December) – Conrad is ill and depressed. In the summer William Rothenstein paints his portrait.

1904 Jessie Conrad suffers a knee injury that leaves her seriously and permanently lame. Conrad's bankers fail. Conrad writes (or, more precisely, dictates to Hueffer) several of the newspaper articles later collected in *The Mirror of the Sea* while continuing work on *Nostromo*, serialization of which has begun in *T.P.'s Weekly* on 29 January. The novel is completed on 30 August, serialization is concluded on 7 October, and it appears in volume form on 14 October. Conrad writes a play, *One Day More*, based on his story 'Tomorrow'. In October the Conrads go to London for about three months so that Jessie may receive treatment.

1905 (7 January) They return to the Pent and then (13 January) leave for a holiday in Capri, where Conrad spends some time with Galsworthy and also meets Norman Douglas. In March he receives a grant of £500 from the Royal Bounty fund. The Conrads leave Capri on 12 May and arrive home on 18 May. In June (25–27), Conrad's one-act play *One Day More* receives five performances at the Royal Court Theatre, London. He finishes 'Gaspar Ruiz' (begun late in 1904), writes 'The Brute', 'The Informer', and 'An Anarchist', and continues work on *Chance*. In December Conrad is 'abominably ill'.

1906   (9 February) The Conrads set off for Montpellier, returning to England on 14 April. While in France Conrad prepares *The Mirror of the Sea* for publication and begins *The Secret Agent*, which is finished by early November, serialization having been begun on 6 October. In May they spend twelve days at Winchelsea, and on 10 July they go to London for about eight weeks. (2 August) Birth of John Conrad. (4 October) Publication of *The Mirror of the Sea*. (4 December) Conrad finishes 'Il Conde'. (16 December) The Conrads again set off for Montpellier; Conrad visits Marguerite Poradowska in Paris.

1907   In Montpellier Conrad works on 'The Duel' (finished on 11 April) and again takes up *Chance*. (12 January) Serialization of *The Secret Agent* is concluded. The children fall ill in France, and the Conrads move to Geneva; meanwhile Conrad is at work revising and expanding *The Secret Agent*. On 12 August they return to England, and on 10 September move to The Someries on the Luton Hoo estate, Bedfordshire. (10 September) *The Secret Agent* is published in volume form. In December Conrad begins *Razumov*, later retitled *Under Western Eyes*.

1908   At the beginning of the year Conrad writes 'The Black Mate', published in the *London Magazine* in April but not collected by Conrad. (6 August) *A Set of Six* published. (December) Conrad contributes the first instalment of *A Personal Record* under the title *Some Reminiscences* to the first number of the *English Review*; serialization continues to June 1909.

1909   (March) The Conrads move to Aldington, Kent. In late November and early December, Conrad writes 'The Secret Sharer'. He continues work on *Under Western Eyes*. During this year he is frequently ill.

1910   (22 January) Conrad finishes *Under Western Eyes*. He falls seriously ill and is laid up for three months. (June) The Conrads move to Capel House, near Ashford, Kent. (October) Conrad meets Frank Harris. During this year he writes 'A Smile of Fortune', 'The Partner', and 'Prince Roman'. Serialization of *Under Western Eyes* begins in the *English Review* and *North American Review* in December.

1911   (February) Conrad finishes 'Freya of the Seven Isles'. He falls ill again. In the summer the *New York Herald* invites him to contribute a serial story, and he works on *Chance*, which he has been writing intermittently during the past six years. On 9 August he is awarded a Civil List pension of one hundred pounds. John Quinn, an American collector, purchases some of his manuscripts. In September he finishes 'A Smile of Fortune' and 'Prince Roman'. (September) Borys Conrad joins the training ship *Worcester*. *Under Western Eyes* is published in volume form on 5 October; serialization is concluded in the same month.

1912   (19 January) *Some Reminiscences*, later retitled *A Personal Record*, is published. (21 January) Serialization of *Chance* begins in the *New York Herald*. (25 March) *Chance* is completed. In May Conrad begins a short story which eventually grows into the novel *Victory*. (14 October) *'Twixt Land and Sea* published. At the end of the year, Conrad writes 'The Inn of the Two Witches'. During this and the following year, Conrad becomes a best-seller, largely thanks to the success of *Chance*. His health continues to be poor: in September he describes his depression as 'awful'. In November Conrad meets Richard Curle.

1913   (September) Conrad meets Bertrand Russell. (18 September) *Chance* appears in volume form. During this year he works at *Victory* and writes 'Because of the Dollars' and 'The Planter of Malata'.

1914   (15 January) *Chance* appears in volume form. Work continues on *Victory*, which is completed by the end of June. (25 July) The Conrads and the Retingers sail from Harwich and travel via Hamburg and Berlin to Cracow (see 'Poland Revisited' in *Notes on Life and Letters*). When war breaks out in August, the Conrads make their way back to England via Vienna, Milan and Genoa, arriving at Tilbury on 3 November.

1915   Early in the year Conrad begins *The Shadow-Line*, which is
        finished by the end of the year. (24 February) Publication
        of *Within the Tides*. (24 September) *Victory*, which has been
        serialized in the *Star* (London) from 24 August, continuing
        until 9 November, appears in volume form.

1916   (May) Death of Conrad's friend Arthur Marwood. (Sep-
        tember) Serialization of *The Shadow-Line* begins in the
        English Review. (November) Conrad goes on H.M.S. *Ready*,
        a sailing vessel engaged in mending torpedo-net defences.
        During this year he writes 'The Warrior's Soul' and 'The
        Tale'.

1917   (19 March) *The Shadow-Line* appears in volume form;
        serialization is concluded in the same month. (Late July)
        Conrad begins a story that later turns into *The Arrow of
        Gold*. In late November they visit London so that Jessie
        may undergo treatment.

1918   (4 June) Conrad finishes *The Arrow of Gold*. In July Conrad
        again takes up *The Rescue*. (December) Serialization of *The
        Arrow of Gold* begins in *Lloyd's Magazine*.

1919   (30 January) Serialization of *The Rescue* begins in *Land and
        Water*, continuing until 31 July. (25 March) The Conrads
        leave Capel House and live in a temporary home, Spring
        Grove, near Wye, Kent. (26 March) First performances of
        a dramatization of *Victory* at the Globe Theatre. (25 May)
        Conrad finishes *The Rescue*, twenty-three years after start-
        ing it. (June) Conrad sells the film rights to his works for
        £3080. (6 August) *The Arrow of Gold* is published in
        volume form. In the autumn Conrad starts work on a
        dramatic version of *The Secret Agent*. (October) The
        Conrads move to Oswalds in the village of Bishopsbourne,
        near Canterbury. In December they spend over three
        weeks in Liverpool, where Jessie undergoes a knee opera-
        tion.

1920   At the beginning of the year Conrad is seriously ill for a
        month, but he works on the proofs of *The Rescue* from
        mid-January until late February. Serialization of *The
        Arrow of Gold* is concluded in February. (March) Conrad
        finishes his dramatization of *The Secret Agent* and writes a
        play, *Laughing Anne*, at this time. He writes the Author's
        Notes for a collected edition of his work. (24 June) *The
        Rescue* is published in volume form. During June Conrad

visits the British Museum to research into the background for *Suspense*.

1921 (23 January) The Conrads leave London for Corsica, travelling through France, where they visit the battlefields near Armentières. They stay in Ajaccio and are joined there by Pinker and his family, returning to England on 10 April. (25 March) *Notes on Life and Letters* appears. Conrad continues work on *Suspense*. Towards the end of the year he begins a novella that develops into *The Rover* (finished on 27 June 1922).

1922 (8 February) Death of J. B. Pinker. (2 November) Conrad's dramatization of *The Secret Agent* opens at the Ambassador's Theatre, London, but runs for only ten performances.

1923 (21 April) Conrad sails from Glasgow on the *Tuscania*, bound for New York, arriving there on 1 May and leaving on 2 June on the liner *Majestic*. On his return he learns that his son Borys had been secretly married on 2 September 1922. (3 December) Publication of *The Rover*.

1924 (January) Conrad sits for a portrait by Walter Tittle (now in the National Portrait Gallery; see Plate 5a). Conrad's grandson Philip is born. (May) Conrad is offered, and declines, a knighthood. (He has earlier declined honorary degrees from five universities.) (3 August) Conrad dies of a heart attack and (7 August) after a funeral service at St Thomas' Roman Catholic Church, Canterbury, is buried in Canterbury cemetery.

1925 (27 June) Serialization of *Suspense* begins in *Hutchinson's Magazine*, continuing to 12 August. The novel is published in volume form on 16 September. (October) Publication of *The Congo Diary*.

1926 Publication of *Last Essays*.

1928 Publication of Conrad's unfinished novel *The Sisters*.

A Conrad Who's Who

BEARD, Elijah.   Captain of the *Palestine*, in which Conrad sailed as second mate in 1881–3: for details of its extraordinary last voyage, see 'A Conrad Chronology'. Although Beard (born 1824) was in his late fifties, it was his first command. Conrad's experiences on the *Palestine* are recounted in 'Youth', in which Beard appears under his own name (though his Christian name is changed to John) and the ship is renamed the *Judea*.

BENNETT, Arnold (1867–1931), English novelist.   His highly successful career as an author formed a curious contrast to that of Conrad. J. B. Pinker, Conrad's literary agent, acted also for Bennett. There are numerous references to Conrad in Bennett's journals and letters. He recognized the excellence of *The Nigger of the 'Narcissus'* when it appeared ('He is so consciously an artist': letter to H. G. Wells, 8 December 1897), and told Conrad in a letter of 22 November 1912 that 'When I first read [*Nostromo*] I thought it was the finest novel of this generation (bar none) and I am still thinking so.' His judgment of *The Secret Agent*, on the other hand, was that it 'gives a disappointing effect of slightness' in comparison with *Nostromo* (journal entry for 25 September 1907).

BLACKWOOD, William (1836–1912), publisher.   As editor of *Blackwood's Magazine* he published some of Conrad's early work, including 'Youth', 'Heart of Darkness' and *Lord Jim*.

BLAKE, Edwin John.   Master of the *Tilkhurst*, in which Conrad sailed to the Far East and back in 1885–6. In *The Mirror of the Sea* he is described.

BOBROWSKA, Teofila (Theophilia).   Conrad's maternal

16

grandmother. She took care of him after he was orphaned at the age of eleven.

BOBROWSKI, Stefan. Conrad's maternal uncle, brother of Tadeusz Bobrowski. He was a member of the Central National Committee, a revolutionary body established in Warsaw to work for Polish independence from Russia, and in 1863 was killed in a duel that probably originated in a political dispute.

BOBROWSKI, Tadeusz (Thaddeus) (1829–94). Conrad's maternal uncle and, after he was orphaned, his guardian, described by Conrad as 'a man of powerful intelligence and great force of character. . . . a most distinguished man to whom I stand more in the relation of a son than of a nephew' (letter to Edward Garnett, 20 January 1900). Bobrowski had studied law at St Petersburg University. He visited Conrad in Marseilles after the putative suicide attempt in 1878. Conrad visited him in Marienbad in 1883 and on his estate near Kiev in 1893. His numerous surviving letters to Conrad are an important source of information; Conrad's side of the correspondence is, however, lost. His *Memoirs* were published in 1900. *Almayer's Folly* is dedicated to his memory, and there are many references to him in *A Personal Record*.

CAPES, Harriet. An early admirer of Conrad, she corresponded with him for many years and compiled *Wisdom and Beauty from Conrad* (1915), *A Set of Six* is dedicated to her.

CASEMENT, Roger (later Sir Roger) (1864–1916). He had a distinguished career in the Consular Service and was knighted in 1911; subsequently he became a fervent Irish nationalist and was hanged for treason. Conrad met him in 1890 at Matadi on the Congo, where Casement later became British Consul, and wrote of him in his diary, 'Thinks, speaks well, most intelligent and very sympathetic.' Baines describes him as 'the only man from the whole Congo episode of whom Conrad spoke with any enthusiasm'. When Casement was accused of treason, however, Conrad refused to sign a petition for a pardon.

CLIFFORD, Hugh. As a young colonial officer in Malaya, he discovered a copy of *Almayer's Folly* in a Singapore bookshop in 1895 and read it enthusiastically. When he returned to England he called on Conrad and became a lifelong friend. Clifford later became colonial secretary of Ceylon and was knighted. Conrad dedicated *Chance* to him. It seems to have been Clifford who set in circulation the story that, before embarking on a career of authorship, Conrad had hesitated between French and English as his medium – a story repeated by Hugh Walpole in his book on Conrad. The story was described by Conrad as 'absurd': in a letter to Walpole he declared that it 'grieves me and makes me dance with rage. . . . When I wrote the first words of *Almayer's Folly* I had been already for years and years *thinking* in English'.

CONRAD, Jessie, née George (1873–1936).   She was working as a typist in London and living in Peckham with her widowed mother when she met Conrad (according to her own account) 'at the end of 1893'. Elsewhere she gives a later date for their first meeting; in a letter of 10 March 1896 Conrad says that he met her 'a year and a half ago'. He describes her in the same letter as 'a small, not at all striking-looking person (to tell the truth alas – rather plain!) who nevertheless is very dear to me'. He proposed to her in February 1896 – her *Joseph Conrad as I Knew Him* (1926) includes an amusing description of his proposal, which she describes as 'surely one of the strangest ever made' – and they were married on 24 March 1896 at a London registry office. *Youth* is dedicated to her, and she is a co-dedicatee of *Romance*. Lady Ottoline Morrell described her as 'a nice and good-looking fat creature, an excellent cook, as Henry James said, and . . . a good and reposeful mattress for this hyper-sensitive, nerve-wrecked man, who did not ask from his wife high intelligence, only an assuagement of life's vibrations' (*Ottoline: the Early Memoirs of Lady Ottoline Morrell*, ed. Robert Gathorne-Hardy [1963] p. 241). In later years Jessie suffered much pain as a result of an accident in 1904 and became very lame. In addition to the book mentioned above, she published *A Handbook of Cookery for a Small House* (1923), to which Conrad contributed a preface (reprinted as 'Cookery' in his *Last Essays*), and *Joseph Conrad and his Circle* (1935). She bore Conrad two sons, Borys, born in 1898 and christened Alfred Borys Konrad Korzeniowski, and John, born in 1906. *The Shadow-Line* is dedicated to Borys, the dedication referring to his war service, and he is also a co-dedicatee of *The Inheritors*. Both sons have published interesting volumes of reminiscences: Borys Conrad's *My Father: Joseph Conrad* (1970), and John Conrad's *Joseph Conrad: Times Remembered* (1981).

CRANE, Stephen (1871–1900), American novelist, best remembered for *The Red Badge of Courage* (1895). He settled in England in the summer of 1897 and met Conrad in October of that year, having been introduced by Heinemann's editor, Sidney Pawling. Crane visited the Conrads in November, and in the following February the Conrad family visited the Cranes at their home near Oxted, Surrey. Crane and his wife later moved to a house near Rye, Sussex. In May 1900 Conrad and Jessie saw Crane off at Dover: he was on his way to the Black Forest in a vain attempt to prolong his life, and died of tuberculosis in the following month. Crane had urged Conrad to collaborate with him on a play, *The Predecessor*, but nothing came of the plan. Conrad wrote a preface for Thomas Beer's *Stephen Crane: a Study in American Letters* (1923) as well as an essay on Crane published in the *London Mercury* in December 1919 and collected in *Notes on Life and Letters*. Crane was apparently one of the very few people who called him Joseph.

CUNNINGHAME GRAHAM, R. B. (1852–1936), Scots writer and traveller. Born of an ancient family and educated at Harrow, Robert Bontine Cunninghame Graham was from 1886 to 1892 a Liberal Member of Parliament. He read 'An Outpost of Progress' in the magazine *Cosmopolis* in June and July 1897 and was so struck by it that he wrote to the author, thereby inaugurating a very important friendship and a significant correspondence. They met in London in December 1897. Baines describes him as 'of all Conrad's friends . . . undoubtedly the closest in temperament', and Arthur Symons reports Conrad as once declaring to him, 'Could you conceive for a moment that I could go on existing if Cunninghame Graham were to die?' Cunninghame Graham's maternal grandmother was Spanish, he spent a considerable period in South America, and in 1878 he married a Chilean. He had Socialist convictions, admired the doctrines of William Morris, and 'was a flamboyant public figure who by 1890 had already been the subject of magazine profiles and political cartoons' (Cedric Watts). He wrote a preface for Conrad's posthumous collection *Tales of Hearsay*. *Joseph Conrad's Letters to Cunninghame Graham*, ed. C. T. Watts (1969) contains 81 letters from the period 1897–1923 and has an interesting introduction giving an account of their friendship. Watts is also the author of a critical biography of Cunninghame Graham (1979).

CURLE, Richard (1883–1969). He reviewed *Under Western Eyes* in the *Manchester Guardian* on 11 October 1911, and in November 1912 published an appreciation of Conrad's work in *Rhythm*. Conrad was greatly pleased with the latter and expressed a wish to meet him; the meeting took place before the end of 1912 and the two men became close friends. Curle's *Joseph Conrad: a Study* (1914) was the first full-length study of Conrad's work and was written with his approval. Its conclusion declares that 'Conrad's day is at hand and once his sun is risen it will not set.' Curle later published *The Last Twelve Years of Joseph Conrad* (1928) and *Joseph Conrad and his Characters* (1957). A collection of 150 of Conrad's letters to him appeared in 1928, and *The Arrow of Gold* is dedicated to him.

DELCOMMUNE, Alexandre. As leader of the Congo exploration party that Conrad joined in 1890, he met Conrad and was on board the *Roi des Belges* with him in August of that year. He is referred to in Conrad's *Congo Diary*. His younger brother Camille was the Belgian manager of the Congo enterprise based at Kinshansa and is depicted as the 'Manager' in *Heart of Darkness* (Conrad had met him in August 1890).

DOUBLEDAY, Frank, American publisher. He stage-managed Conrad's visit to the USA in 1923. Conrad stayed at Doubleday's home on Long Island and accompanied him on a motor tour of New England.

DOUGLAS, Norman (1868–1952), English author. Conrad struck up a friendship with him when he visited Capri, where Douglas was a resident, in 1905, and they subsequently corresponded. At the time Douglas was little known as an author, and Conrad helped him to get his work published.

ELLIS, Captain Henry (died 1908). Master-Attendant (that is, in charge of the port) at Singapore, he 'gave Conrad his first command' and was 'a well-known character in Singapore at the time' (Norman Sherry). Conrad met him only once, and briefly, in January 1888; by the time he returned to Singapore from Bangkok, Ellis had retired (see the end of *The Shadow-Line*). Ellis was the prototype of Captain Ellis in *The Shadow-Line* and of Captain Eliott in *Lord Jim* and 'The End of the Tether' (it may be significant that Conrad used Ellis's actual name for a fictional purpose only after his death). As Sherry points out,
    Conrad's single interview with Ellis attains some prominence

in his work, for it appears in different forms in two stories, and so is an example of Conrad's use of a very slight experience. In *Lord Jim* and *The Shadow-Line* the Master-Attendant is shown interviewing a seaman in his room at the Harbour Office. In *Lord Jim* the seaman is the renegade master of the Patna and in *The Shadow-Line* he is the narrator of the story, obviously Conrad himself. *The Shadow-Line* version is, consequently, the nearest to the facts of Conrad's experience of Ellis. (*Conrad's Eastern World*, p. 196).

EPSTEIN, Jacob (1880–1959), sculptor, executed a bust of Conrad that has been described as 'the most powerful visual image made of Conrad during his lifetime' (Frederick R. Karl).   Conrad sat for Epstein in his own home in March and April 1924, only a few months before his death. In his autobiography, *Let There Be Sculpture* (1940), Epstein recalls his impressions of Conrad:

Conrad was an absorbing study. He took posing seriously and gave me good long sittings until one o'clock, when we lunched and talked. Conrad from the beginning called me Cher Maître, embarrassing me by this mode of address from a much older man who was a great master of his own craft. His manners were courtly and direct, but his neurasthenia forced him at times to outbursts of rage and irritability with his household which quickly subsided. I already had a fairly clear notion as to how I should treat the bust. A sculptor had previously made a bust of him which represented him as an open-necked, romantic, out-of-door type of person. In appearance Conrad was the very opposite. His clothes were immaculately conventional, and his collar enclosed his neck like an Iron Maiden's vice or garrotter's grip. He was worried if his hair and beard were not trim and neat as became a sea captain. There was nothing shaggy or Bohemian about him. His glance was keen despite the drooping of one eyelid. He was the sea captain, the officer, and in our talks he emphasised the word "responsibility". Responsibility weighed on him and weighed him down. He used the word again and again and one immediately thought of *Lord Jim* – the conscience suffering at the evasion of duty. It may have been because of my meeting him late in life that Conrad gave me a feeling of defeat; but defeat met with courage.

He was crippled with rheumatism, crochety, nervous, and ill.
He said to me, "I am finished". There was pathos in his pulling
out of a drawer his last manuscript to show me that he was still
at work. There was no triumph in his manner, however, and he
said that he did not know whether he would ever finish it. "I am
played out," he said, "played out." (pp. 90–1)

FORD, Ford Madox (1873–1939), novelist and critic. Of
Anglo-German parentage and originally named Hueffer, he
changed his name at the end of the Great War. He met Conrad at
the home of Edward Garnett in September 1898, and they
subsequently collaborated on *The Inheritors* (1901) and *Romance*
(1903). Pent Farm, where the Conrads lived 1898–1907, was
rented from Hueffer. After the completion of *Lord Jim* he
accompanied the Conrads on a visit to Belgium. In 1908 Hueffer
founded *The English Review*, which became an influential literary
journal and published *Under Western Eyes* and *The Shadow-Line* as
well as their collaborative effort *The Nature of a Crime*. For Ford's
part in the conception of *The Secret Agent*, see the 'Author's Note' to
that novel. In his *Joseph Conrad: a Personal Remembrance* (1924) Ford
claimed that 'Amy Foster' was 'a short story originally by the
writer [i.e. Ford himself] which Conrad took over and entirely
rewrote'. Jessie Conrad vehemently denied this claim, but
mentioned that Ford had pointed out to Conrad in Winchelsea
churchyard 'a grave which bears on the head-stone no name, but
recording the fact that the bodies of one or two foreign seamen are
buried there, after being washed ashore'. In his book *The Cinque
Ports* Ford included an anecdote, set on Romney Marsh, of a
shipwrecked sailor who could speak no English. (See also
pp. 148–9.)

There is material on Conrad in Ford's critical book *The English
Novel* (1919) and in his volume of memoirs *It Was the Nightingale*
(1933); see also *Letters of Ford Madox Ford*, ed. Richard M. Ludwig
(Princeton, 1965). In his *Return to Yesterday* (1932) Ford describes
Conrad as follows:

He was rather short and round-shouldered with his head as it
were sunken into his body. He had a dark retreating face with a
very carefully trimmed and pointed beard, a trouble–wrinkled
forehead and very troubled dark eyes, and the gestures of his
hands and arms were from the shoulders and very Oriental
indeed. (p. 52)

Arthur Mizener, Ford's biographer, writes that 'Ford provided moral support for Conrad in two ways. He kept Conrad's spirits up by constantly assuring him of what he quite sincerely believed, that Conrad was a great writer. He also took over, in a way that appeared at least to Conrad very effective, many of the practical operations of Conrad's life' (*The Saddest Story: A Biography of Ford Madox Ford* [1971] p. 46). As a novelist, Ford is an important figure in his generation and a major technical innovator; on his relationship to Conrad as a novelist see Thomas Moser, 'Conrad and *The Good Soldier*', in *Joseph Conrad: A Commemoration*, ed. Norman Sherry (1976).

GALSWORTHY, John (1867–1933), English novelist and dramatist. With his friend and fellow-Harrovian Edward Sanderson (see below), Galsworthy was a passenger on the *Torrens* when it set sail from Adelaide in March 1893 with Conrad as chief officer. In a letter written during the voyage to Cape Town, Galsworthy described Conrad as 'a capital chap, though queer to look at; he . . . has a fund of yarns on which I draw freely'. They later became close friends and corresponded frequently. For Galsworthy the man, Conrad had a strong affection, but his view of Galsworthy as a writer is less unambiguous. He dedicated *Nostromo* to him. Galsworthy included some reminiscences of Conrad in his *Castles in Spain and Other Screeds* (1927). He writes there: 'He stared life very much in the face, and distrusted those who didn't. . . . He laughed at the clichés of so-called civilization. His sense of humour, indeed, was far greater than one might think from his work. He had an almost ferocious enjoyment of the absurd.' He also comments that Conrad lived quietly in the country and seldom went to London: 'He wrote always with blood and tears and needed seclusion for it.'

GARNETT, Edward (1868–1937), critic and man of letters. As reader for the publisher Fisher Unwin, in 1894 he recommended the publication of *Almayer's Folly*. He met Conrad in October of that year and (according to Conrad) suggested that he write another novel. During the composition of *An Outcast of the Islands*, he gave Conrad much advice, as he again did over *The Nigger of the 'Narcissus'* and other early works. Conrad's debt to Garnett's literary counsel was considerable and frequently acknowledged. On 19 June 1896 he told him: 'I believe in you – in you as a last refuge, somewhat as an unintelligent and hopeless sinner believes in the infinite mercy on high.' On 24 August 1897 he wrote: 'the *Nigger* is *your* book and besides you know very well I daren't make any move without your knowledge'. Responding to Garnett's favourable review of *The Secret Agent* in October 1907, he wrote: 'Twelve years now – just a round dozen my dear – since I hear your voice in my ear as I put aside each written page. A great affection and an absolute confidence'. Near the end of his life (August 1923) Conrad told Garnett: 'How much you have done to pull me together intellectually only the Gods that brought us together know'; the same letter pays affectionate tribute to their friendship of nearly thirty years' standing. Garnett frequently reviewed Conrad's work, and his reviews, of which several are reprinted in *Critical Heritage*, are important items of early Conrad criticism. His article in *Academy* (15 October 1898) was the first general discussion of Conrad's work to appear. Conrad wrote an introduction to Garnett's *Turgenev: A Study* (1917), collected in *Notes on Life and Letters*. Garnett edited *Letters from Conrad, 1895–1924* (1928). *The Nigger of the 'Narcissus'* is dedicated to him. There is a chapter on Conrad in George Jefferson's *Edward Garnett: A Life in Literature* (1982). Garnett's wife Constance was a well-known translator of Russian literature; Conrad particularly admired her versions of Turgenev. The Garnetts lived at The Cearne, near Limpsfield, Surrey, from 1896; their home became a meeting-place for men of letters, including Conrad.

GIDE, André (1869–1951), French author. He was introduced to Conrad by Agnes Tobin (see below) in July 1911 and subsequently corresponded with him. Gide supervised the translation of Conrad's works into French. See Frederick Karl, 'Conrad and Gide: A Relationship and a Correspondence', *Comparative Literature*, XXIX (1977), pp. 148–71. Ian Watt has noted the significance of the fact that Gide's favourite among Conrad's novels was *Lord Jim*:

. . . it was its 'despairing nobility' that he singled out for admiration. This gives a particular significance to a letter in which Gide told Conrad that if he were ever to write an article about him it would be to Alfred de Vigny and 'to him alone, that I would wish to establish your kinship'. Like Conrad, Alfred de Vigny was a nobleman, a stoic, and a disillusioned romantic; both men combined deeply isolated natures with an emphasis on a collective ethic which had its roots in their careers of professional service ... (*Conrad in the Nineteenth Century*, p. 355).

HALLOWES, Lilian.   Conrad's typist from about 1907 to the end of his life.

HARRIS, Frank (1856–1931), English author and editor.   He met Conrad in 1910 and included reminiscences of him in his *My Life and Loves* (1923–9). His first impressions of Conrad's appearance are recalled thus: 'I had thought from his photograph that his forehead was high and domed, but it was rather low and sloped back quickly. He was a little above middle height and appeared more the student than a sea-captain. Both he and his wife were homely, hospitable folk, without a trace of affectation.'

HENLEY, W. E. (1849–1903), English poet and editor.   Sidney Pawling (see below) showed him the uncompleted manuscript of *The Nigger of the 'Narcissus'* towards the end of 1896, and his reaction was encouraging; he later serialized it in the *New Review*. Henley was an influential figure in the world of letters in the 1890s, and when he accepted the *Nigger* Conrad wrote, 'Now I have conquered Henley I ain't 'fraid of the divvle himself.' Later he described Henley as 'a horrible bourgeois'.

HODISTER, Arthur.   Possible and partial prototype for Kurtz in *Heart of Darkness* (see also entry for Klein below). Roger Tennant writes:

> In so far as Conrad had any external source [for Kurtz], it would seem to be an adventurous Belgian agent called Hodister, whom he never met, but of whom he may well have heard envious gossip such as Marlow hears of Kurtz. Like Conrad and Kurtz, Hodister had influential connections in Brussels. . . . An eloquent opponent of the slave trade, and a highly successful collector of ivory, he was eventually killed in a tribal war in Katanga incited by rival Belgian and Arab interests, and had his own head put on a post in the manner that Kurtz, in the story, treats his victims. . . . It seems clear, however, that he was simply a brave, intelligent adventurer, with none of the Nietzschean complexities of Conrad's creation.
> (*Joseph Conrad* [1981], p. 80)

Norman Sherry argues in detail in *Conrad's Western World* (pp. 95–118) that Hodister and Kurtz shared a number of characteristics. Ian Watt points out, however, that there were 'many important differences between them' and that in any case there were 'many partial similarities between Kurtz and numerous other people who were in the Congo during the period' (*Conrad and the Nineteenth Century*, p. 142).

HOPE, G. W. F.   He served as apprentice on the wool clipper *Duke of Sutherland*, on which Conrad had sailed to Australia and back in 1878–9, and this gave them a basis for friendship when they met in London in 1880. Hope had become director of a South African mining company and was a keen amateur yachtsman; Conrad often accompanied him on trips on the Thames in Hope's boat *Nellie* (referred to on the opening page of *Heart of Darkness*, where Hope appears as 'The Director of Companies . . . our Captain and our host'). He was a witness at Conrad's wedding, and *Lord Jim* is dedicated to Hope and his wife. Hope later noted that on their first meeting Conrad spoke 'very broken English'.

HUDSON, W. H. (1841–1922), author.   Born in Argentina of American parents, he settled in England in 1869. The merits of his work were recognized by Edward Garnett (see above), who helped to establish him as a writer. He and Conrad met occasionally but their friendship does not seem to have been a close one.

HUEFFER: see Ford.

JAMES, Henry (1843–1916), novelist.   In October 1896 Conrad sent James a flatteringly inscribed copy of *An Outcast of the Islands*, and James responded with a copy of *The Spoils of Poynton* and an invitation to lunch; they met for the first time at James's London home on 25 February 1897. After Ford Madox Ford moved to Winchelsea (Sussex) in 1901, Conrad visited him frequently and often called on James, who was living in the nearby town of Rye. In 1902 James supported the attempt to obtain a grant for Conrad from the Royal Literary Fund. According to James's biographer Leon Edel, 'James extravagantly praised Conrad's early work. The middle period – *Nostromo*, *The Secret Agent*, *Under Western Eyes* – he described to [Edith] Wharton as "impossibilities" and a "waste of desolation that succeeded the two or three final good things of his earlier time". *Chance* he found "rather yieldingly difficult and charming".' In an article on the contemporary novel, 'The Younger Generation', published in the *Times Literary Supplement* in 1914 and reprinted in his *Notes on Novelists* (1931) under the title 'The New Novel', James praised Conrad but expressed reservations concerning the technique of *Chance*. Conrad later said that the article was 'the only time a criticism affected me painfully' (letter of 24 May 1916). After James' death, Conrad said that he had 'a profound affection for him'. He published an essay on James in the *North American Review* in January 1905, collected in *Notes on Life and Letters*.

JEAN-AUBRY, G.   Friend and first biographer of Conrad. His two-volume *Joseph Conrad: Life and Letters* (1927) contains many letters and much information obtained at first hand from Conrad, but has been largely superseded by the later biographies by Baines, Karl, and Najder, as has Jean-Aubry's *The Sea Dreamer: A Definitive Biography of Joseph Conrad* (1957; French edition, 1947). He also published *Conrad au Congo* (1925; translated 1926).

KLEIN, Georges Antoine.   An agent of the Belgian Congo exploitation company, he joined the *Roi des Belges* at Stanley Falls for the return journey to Kinshasa in September 1890 but, already seriously ill with dysentery at the start of the voyage, he died on board (21 September). In the manuscript of *Heart of Darkness* the name of Kurtz (German for 'short') was first given as Klein (German for 'small'); and when Conrad was asked in an interview in 1923 whether Kurtz was based on an actual person, he remarked, 'I saw him die.' However, in spite of his claim in the 'Author's Note' that the story records 'experience pushed a little (and only very little) beyond the actual facts of the case', the parallel between Kurtz and Klein seems slight. Ian Watt concludes that 'Klein was no Kurtz', but suggests that

merely 'seeing him die' gave Conrad an unbearably painful memory. From the departure on September 6th until Klein's death 15 days later, there would, in the very cramped quarters of the *Roi des Belges*, have been no escape from the sounds, the smells and the sight of a man in the last stages of dysentery – a disease peculiarly repulsive in its physical manifestations, and usually marked by an unimaginable degree of emaciation; this may have supplied Marlow's description of Kurtz: 'the cage of his ribs all astir, the bones of his arm waving . . . an animated image of death carved out of old ivory'. (*Conrad in the Nineteenth Century*, p. 142)

See also the entry for Hodister above.

KORZENIOWSKI, Apollo (1820–69). The father of Joseph Conrad and the son of Teodor Korzeniowski (see below). Born in the Ukraine, he studied at the University of St Petersburg and became a poet and playwright: among other works, he translated Dickens' *Hard Times*, Shakespeare's *Comedy of Errors* and de Vigny's *Chatterton* into Polish, and wrote a poem on his son's birth and another on his baptism. After a long courtship and in the face of bitter opposition from her family, he married Ewa Bobrowska (see Ewa Korzeniowska below) on 8 May 1856. He became involved in revolutionary politics. In 1861 he went to Warsaw to edit a new literary magazine, was arrested in October of that year, and was sentenced by the court to exile 'in forced residence and under police supervision' (Morf), his wife sharing the sentence. On 8 May 1862 they left with their four-year-old son for Vologda, north of Moscow, spending over a month on the journey, during which time both the child and his mother fell ill. In Vologda, Apollo contracted tuberculosis and applied for permission to move to a warmer climate; in the summer of 1863, the family settled in Chernikov, near Kiev, where Apollo worked on translations of Shakespeare, Dickens and Victor Hugo. In January 1868 he left Russia for Lwow (Lemberg) in Galicia. He died on 23 May 1869 in Cracow (see *A Personal Record*). His funeral is described in the 'Author's Note' to *A Personal Record* and in the essay 'Poland Revisited', collected in *Notes on Life and Letters*.

KORZENIOWSKA, Ewa (Ewelina), née Bobrowska (1833–65). Wife of the above and mother of Joseph Conrad. In 1863 she was allowed to interrupt her exile in order to visit her brother Tadeusz Bobrowski (see above), and her son accompanied her on this visit. Although dangerously ill, she was forced to return: for an account of this episode see *A Personal Record*, where Conrad recalls her 'dressed in the black of the national mourning worn in defiance of ferocious police regulations'. She died on 18 April 1865.

KORZENIOWSKI, Teodor. Paternal grandfather of Conrad. He served as a cavalry officer and then 'retired to a little hereditary estate' (letter to Edward Garnett, 20 January 1900). Conrad also states that he 'wrote a tragedy in five acts, privately printed, and so extremely dull that no one was ever known to have read it through'.

KRIEGER, Adolf. One of the two close friends of Conrad's early days in England (the other was G. W. F. Hope: see above). Krieger was an American of German parentage and was employed by a firm of shipping agents. He and Conrad met in 1880 and occupied the same lodgings in Holloway, North London, while Conrad was preparing for the examination to qualify him as second mate. During his later visits to London, Conrad often stayed with Krieger and his wife at their Stoke Newington home, and it was Krieger who acted as agent for the transfer of funds to Conrad from his uncle and who in 1891 found Conrad a job in a London warehouse. Eventually the two men quarrelled over a debt owed by Conrad to Krieger. Norman Sherry suggests that Krieger was a model for Verloc in *The Secret Agent*. Krieger was one of the witnesses at Conrad's wedding, and *Tales of Unrest* is dedicated to him 'for the sake of old days'.

LINGARD, William. A ship's captain and trader in the East, he was the 'original' of Captain Tom Lingard in *Almayer's Folly*, *An Outcast of the Islands* and *The Rescue*. His nephew Jim worked at his uncle's trading post at Berau in Borneo with Charles Olmeijer (see below). Norman Sherry writes in *Conrad's Eastern World* (p. 133): 'It seems clear to me that the whole complex of Lingard's relatives and protégés . . . fascinated Conrad, and he shuffled the relationships about a little each time he made use of them so as to obtain a slightly different perspective for each novel.' Sherry regards it as unlikely that Conrad ever met William Lingard and suggests that he depended on oral tradition for his knowledge of Lingard's life and career.

MARRIS, Charles. Half-Maori sailor resident in Penang and married to a Malayan. At one time he had commanded the *Vidar*, on which Conrad served (under another captain) in 1887. Marris visited Conrad in England in 1909, and their conversation about Eastern places and personalities seems to have stimulated Conrad to write the three stories collected in *'Twixt Land and Sea*, which is dedicated to Marris.

MARWOOD, Arthur (died 1916). The younger son of a baronet and 'a cultured right-wing radical of the kind that Conrad found most congenial' (Tennant), he was introduced to Conrad by Ford in about 1906 and became a close friend. He is said to be the prototype of Mills in *The Arrow of Gold* as well as of Ford's Tietjens in his *Parade's End*.

MORRELL, Lady Ottoline (1873–1938).   Wife of an MP and hostess at her homes in London and Oxfordshire to a notable circle of writers, artists and intellectuals. Accompanied by Bertrand Russell (see below), she visited Conrad at his Kent home in 1912 and later recorded her impressions of the visit. She describes his appearance as

> really that of a Polish nobleman. His manner was perfect, almost too elaborate; so nervous and sympathetic that every fibre of him seemed electric, which gave him the air of a highly-polished and well-bred man.
>
> He talked English with a strong accent, as if he tasted his words in his mouth before pronouncing them; but he talked extremely well, though he had always the talk and manner of a foreigner. It seemed difficult to believe that this charming gentleman with high square shoulders, which he shrugged now and again so lightly, and the unmistakably foreign look, had been a captain in the English Merchant Service, and was, too, such a master of English prose. (*Ottoline: the Early Memoirs of Lady Ottoline Morrell*, pp. 239–40)

Lady Ottoline records that the conversation, among other topics, touched on 'the horrors of the Congo', and that Conrad 'talked with great admiration of Henry James'.

NORTHCLIFFE, Viscount (born Alfred Harmsworth) (1865–1922).   Newspaper proprietor; towards the end of his life he became friendly with Conrad.

OLMEIJER, William Charles.   In 1887 Conrad made four brief trips in the steamer *Vidar* to Berau, a trading-post in Eastern Borneo, and there came across Olmeijer, a half-caste manager who had been there for some seventeen or eighteen years as the representative of Captain William Lingard (see above). Olmeijer became the prototype of Kaspar Almayer in *Almayer's Folly* and *An Outcast of the Islands*. In *A Personal Record*, which includes a description of Olmeijer, Conrad wrote: 'If I had not got to know Almayer pretty well it is almost certain there would never have been a line of mine in print.' He cannot have known Olmeijer well, and the precise relationship between fact and fiction is impossible to determine; the problem is thoroughly examined in Norman Sherry's *Conrad's Eastern World*. See also the section on *Almayer's Folly* later in this volume.

PADEREWSKI, Jan (1860–1941). Distinguished pianist and composer; he became the first prime minister of Poland in 1919. Conrad met him in New York in 1923; his subsequent visit to Conrad's home in England is described in John Conrad's memoir of his father.

PAWLING, Sidney (1862–1923). As partner in the publishing firm of Heinemann he became interested in the uncompleted manuscript of *The Nigger of the 'Narcissus'* towards the end of 1896 (it had been shown to him by Edward Garnett), and later recommended its acceptance by Heinemann. Pawling also showed it to the editor W. E. Henley (see above).

PINKER, J. B. (1863–1922). One of the first and most notable members of the profession of literary agent, he acted for Conrad from the turn of the century and handled his work from 'Typhoon' onwards. When Pinker died, Conrad said he felt the loss 'profoundly', spoke of their intimacy during the war years as 'very close', and described him as 'my friend of twenty years' standing, whose devotion to my interests and whose affection borne towards myself and all belonging to me were the greatest moral and material support through nearly all my writing life' (letter of 19 February 1922). They had nevertheless quarrelled at the beginning of 1910 and had been estranged for nearly two years. Conrad's correspondence with Pinker (nearly 1300 letters) shows that he frequently sought his aid at times of financial crisis. Conrad's letters to Pinker (1899–1922) have been described by Frederick R. Karl as 'Conrad's true autobiography, an inner journey related in the epistolary style'. See also Karl's 'Conrad and Pinker' in *Joseph Conrad: A Commemoration*, ed. Norman Sherry (1976).

PORADOWSKI, Aleksander. A cousin of Conrad's maternal grandmother, he escaped from Poland after the 1863 insurrection, eventually settled in Belgium, and married Marguerite Gachet, a Frenchwoman who became an authoress and the confidante and correspondent of Conrad. In February 1890, Conrad visited Aleksander, who was on his deathbed, and met Marguerite Poradowska. Conrad's side of their correspondence was published in 1940 as *Letters of Joseph Conrad to Marguerite Poradowska*. The volume contains 92 letters from the period 1890–95 and a further 18 letters from 1900–20. Marguerite visited the Conrads in

Kent in April 1900. She died in Paris in 1937 at the age of 89. Conrad referred to her as an aunt, but this was a purely honorary title.

QUINN, John (died 1924). American collector introduced to Conrad by Agnes Tobin; he bought many of Conrad's manuscripts at a time when Conrad desperately needed the money, and sold them by auction in 1923.

RETINGER, Joseph. Polish patriot: Conrad met him in 1912. Retinger persuaded him to support the cause of Polish independence and to take his family on a visit to Poland in 1914 in the company of Retinger and his wife Otalia. He published *Conrad and his Contemporaries: Souvenirs* (1941), which Najder describes as 'lively, scintillating, witty, and seldom reliable'.

ROTHENSTEIN, William (1872–1945). English artist who painted portraits of Conrad and his son Borys and who was a regular visitor to Conrad's home. Rothenstein published three volumes of memoirs containing many references to Conrad; an abridged version has been published as *Men and Memories: Recollections, 1872–1938*, ed. Mary Lago (Columbia, Missouri, 1978). On 12 July 1904 Rothenstein wrote to Edmund Gosse that 'Conrad told me some little time ago that his earnings during the 10 years he has been writing were £1400'. He adds: 'I have borrowed £150 for him, to which I have myself added £50, to ease his immediate difficulties, and I am trying to get £300 more, to put his affairs on a proper basis' (quoted in *Men and Memories*, pp. 143–4).

RUSSELL, Bertrand (1872–1970). English mathematician and philosopher. He met Conrad in September 1913 when he visited Capel House with Lady Ottoline Morrell (see above). Later in the same month Conrad visited Russell in Cambridge. They corresponded, and Russell named his son John Conrad and expressed the wish that Conrad might regard himself as a kind of unofficial godfather. *The Autobiography of Bertrand Russell, 1872–1914* (1967) contains a very striking passage on Conrad (pp. 207–10) in which Russell states that 'My relation to Joseph Conrad was unlike any other that I have ever had. . . . In the out-works of our lives, we were almost strangers, but we shared a certain outlook on human life and human destiny, which, from the very first, made a bond of extreme strength'. He refers to Conrad's 'love of England and hatred of Russia', and quotes from a letter in which Conrad expressed towards himself 'A deep admiring affection which, if you were never to see me again and forgot my existence tomorrow, would be unalterably yours *usque ad finem*'. Russell's *Portraits from Memory and Other Essays* (1956) also contains interesting material on Conrad.

SANDERSON, Edward (died 1939).   For Sanderson's meeting with Conrad, see the entry for Galsworthy above. In 1894, Conrad visited the Sandersons at their home in Elstree; later he dedicated *The Mirror of the Sea* to Mrs Katherine Sanderson, Edward's mother, 'whose warm welcome and gracious hospitality cheered the first dark days of my parting with the sea'. According to one account, Sanderson and his mother encouraged Conrad to seek publication for *Almayer's Folly* and helped him to correct the English in his manuscript. Sanderson and his wife Helen remained lifelong friends of Conrad.

SHAW, George Bernard (1856–1950), dramatist. He was introduced to Conrad by H. G. Wells and paid a visit to him in 1902.

TOBIN, Agnes, minor American poetess.   She was introduced to Conrad by Arthur Symons, the poet and editor, in 1911, and *Under Western Eyes* was later dedicated to her. She introduced André Gide and John Quinn (see entries above) to Conrad.

WALPOLE, Hugh (1884–1941).   In 1916 he published one of the earliest books on Conrad (revised edition 1924), but the two men did not meet until 1918. On that occasion (23 January) Walpole wrote in his diary:
> Conrad even better than I had expected – looking older, very nervous, rather fantastic and dramatic somehow – his eyes I think – 'an intellectual Corsair'. He talked eagerly, telling me all kinds of things about his early life. Delighted when I said I liked *Nostromo* best, although he said *The Nigger* was *the* book!

A friendship developed, and Conrad later wrote a preface for an anthology of Walpole's work (1922). Rupert Hart-Davis's biography of Walpole (1952) contains numerous references to Conrad.

WELLS, H. G. (1866–1946), novelist and critic.   His review of *An Outcast of the Islands* in the *Saturday Review* in May 1896 gave rise to a correspondence with Conrad; and when the Conrads moved to Pent Farm in 1898 they became neighbours of Wells, who was living in Kent (at Sandgate). The two writers soon met, became friends, and exchanged books. Conrad dedicated *The Secret Agent* to Wells. Subsequently, however, for reasons that are unclear but may well have been related to profound differences of outlook, the friendship cooled. In his diary Hugh Walpole quoted Conrad as saying, 'The difference between us, Wells, is fundamental. You don't care for humanity but think they are to be improved. I love humanity but know they are not!' For Wells' account of Conrad, see his *Experiment in Autobiography* (1934).

WILLIAMS, Augustine Podmore (1852–1916). Chief officer of the *Jeddah*, the ship on which Conrad based the *Patna* in *Lord Jim* (for further details of the notorious *Jeddah* case of 1880, see the section on that novel later in this volume). Norman Sherry (in *Conrad's Eastern World*) argues persuasively that Williams is a prototype of both Jim (in *Lord Jim*) and Leggatt (in 'The Secret Sharer'). Like Jim, he was a parson's son and became a water-clerk in Singapore after the court of inquiry (at which period Conrad may have met him); and like Jim he married a Eurasian. Unlike Jim, however, he did not jump from the *Jeddah* but 'had his hand wounded and was flung into the sea by the pilgrims, being picked up by the captain'; and unlike Jim he remained in Singapore to the end of his days. Arguing that Conrad met Williams in Singapore, Sherry comments: 'it is apparent that Conrad's inspiration depended upon a much closer contact with his source than he indicates in the Author's Note to *Lord Jim*'.

Conrad's World

POLAND

Conrad spent his first sixteen years in Poland, from his birth on 3 December 1857 until his departure for Marseilles on 15 October 1874, with two substantial interruptions: the period of his father's exile in Russia (May 1862–January 1868, with visits to his uncle Tadeusz during this time), and the months he spent in Switzerland in 1873. Since the late eighteenth century, Poland had been partitioned between Austria, Prussia and Russia. Conrad was born in Russian-occupied Poland, at Berdyczów, south-west of Kiev and about 110 miles north of the Derebczynka estate, which was leased and farmed by his father. (Baines, Karl and others have given his birthplace as Derebczynka Manor, but Najder (p. 10) has shown that this is incorrect.) During the boy's second year, his family moved to Zhitomir, a little to the north-east, and then two years later to Warsaw, in the region occupied by Austria. When his father was allowed to return to Poland from exile at the beginning of 1868, the widower and his young son settled in Lvov (Lemberg) in Galicia, not far from Conrad's birthplace; and after his father's death in the following year the boy continued to live in Austrian-occupied Poland and received some education at schools in Lvov and Cracow.

In later years, Conrad returned twice to Poland: once in 1890, just before his experiences in the Congo, when he visited his uncle Tadeusz, and again on the eve of the Great War, when he took his wife and sons (see 'Poland Revisited' in *Notes on Life and Letters*).

The bitterness of his early years, which had brought the insecurities of exile and the death of both of his parents, perhaps provides sufficient reason for Conrad's decision to leave Poland.

35

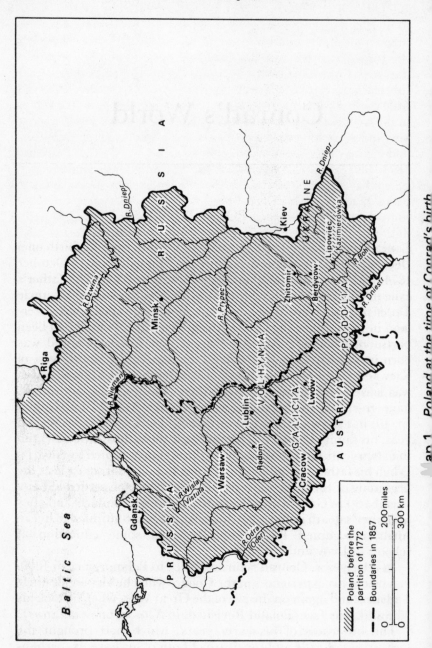

Map 1 *Poland at the time of Conrad's birth*

Frederick R. Karl has suggested that a gifted and energetic young man would have found himself profoundly out of sympathy with the prevailing mood of his surviving family, whose lives were 'devoted almost completely to reliving the tragedies of the past, the death of relatives, of personal hopes, and of Poland; there was little room in which to live. For a young man of sixteen, they faced in the wrong direction'. Since he had conceived the desire to go to sea, and since for educated Poles French was a second language and France a favourite country of exile, the move to Marseilles in 1874 was logical and almost inevitable. But the severance of ties, patriotic, linguistic and familial, clearly made a profound and permanent impression upon him; he wrote of 'taking a standing jump out of his racial surroundings and associations', and the figure who 'jumps' out of an established pattern of life, whether from cowardice or for some other reason, is a recurring one in his fiction. Several of his Polish critics in particular have regarded Conrad as guilt-haunted by his desertion of Poland, and in *A Personal Record* Conrad himself uses that loaded and disturbing word: he asks there why he should have quitted the land of his ancestors in order to

undertake the pursuit of fantastic meals of salt junk and hard tack upon the wide seas? On the kindest view it seems an unanswerable question. Alas! I have the conviction that there are men of unstained rectitude who are ready to murmur scornfully the word desertion.

Conrad also observes in *A Personal Record* that 'No charge of faithlessness ought to be lightly uttered. . . . The fidelity to a special tradition may last through the events of an unrelated existence, following faithfully, too, the traced way of an inexplicable impulse.' That 'fidelity' has been endorsed by Ian Watt, who in *Conrad in the Nineteenth Century* argues that Conrad remained

deeply devoted to the idea of national sentiment; unlike the other great figures of modern literature, Conrad was not the critic but the nostalgic celebrant of the civilization of his homeland; and the steady insistence on the patriotic values of courage, tenacity, honour, responsibility and abnegation gives Conrad's fiction a heroic note very rare in twentieth-century literature.

Watt also points out that in his later years, living in England with an English wife, Conrad retained much of the outlook and even the lifestyle of a Polish landowner, approximating 'as far as means permitted, to that of the country gentleman'. A Polish friend described him in 1909 as 'a typical Polish landowner from the Ukraine', and accounts by contemporaries emphasize the unmistakable foreignness of his speech and gestures, and even of his dress, after many years' residence in England.

FRANCE

Conrad stayed in France for about three and a half years, from the age of sixteen until he was twenty, but was away during that period for three voyages to the West Indies. No letters survive from these years, and little is known for certain about his experiences or relationships. During 1877 it is possible – though far from certain, and Najder indeed regards it as 'highly questionable if not impossible' – that he was involved in gun-running to Spain; and early in the following year he received a wound in the chest which he later claimed (and may have come to believe) was the result of a duel but which was evidently the result of a half-hearted and perhaps deliberately unsuccessful suicide attempt. (Ian Watt comments that to have remembered the suicide attempt as a duel 'would only be an extreme example of Conrad's general tendency in his later years to reconstruct the past in a flattering and romantic way'). His Marseilles experiences, including the putative gun-running and duel, formed the basis of his late novel *The Arrow of Gold*. Another late novel, *The Rover*, also draws on his recollections of the south of France.

The Conrads spent their prolonged honeymoon in Brittany in 1896 (details in 'A Conrad Chronology'), and the short story 'The Idiots' written at that time uses a local setting. In later years they spent holidays in France, including two visits to Montpellier in 1906–7.

To return to his youthful residence there: once he had been extricated from his financial and other troubles by his uncle Tadeusz, Conrad resolved to leave France, and the problem arose where he was to go next. To return to Poland would have made him liable for military service under the Russians, and in any case he had by this time determined to follow the profession of sailor.

According to *A Personal Record* he had long resolved 'if a seaman, then an English seaman'; whether or not this is true, his next move was to join a British ship and eventually to make his way to England.

ENGLAND

According to his own account, Conrad heard his first words of spoken English on board the *Mavis*, a British steamer which he joined in Marseilles in April 1878 for a voyage to the eastern Mediterranean; a couple of months later, when the *Mavis* arrived in Lowestoft harbour, he set foot on English soil for the first time, at the age of twenty. He visited London at this time, and again in October of the same year. Between the two visits he made three trips between Lowestoft and Newcastle on another boat.

For the next fifteen years the pattern of Conrad's life is one of voyages, mainly lengthy voyages to the Far East and Australia, with relatively short periods in England between them. In 1880, for instance, he spent nearly seven months in London studying for his second mate's certificate; in 1886 he spent several months there studying for, and taking (twice) the examination for, his master's certificate; and in 1891 he was intermittently in London – partly in hospital, recovering from the effects of his visit to the Congo, and partly working in a warehouse. (For details of the various voyages and the periods between them, see 'A Conrad Chronology'.)

The two voyages to Australia on the *Torrens* were Conrad's last of any importance, and with the acceptance for publication of *Almayer's Folly* in 1894 he was launched on his second and landbound career of authorship. For the rest of his life, however, in his various homes in Essex and Kent, he was never far from the sea.

During his brief periods in London, Conrad lived in various furnished lodgings (see Hans van Marle, 'Conrad's English Lodgings', *Conradiana*, 1976). In 1879, for instance, he was in Tollington Park Street, Finsbury Park, and later at 6 Dynevor Road, Stoke Newington. In 1889–90 he lived in Bessborough Gardens, Pimlico, near Vauxhall Bridge; and it was there that he began to write *Almayer's Folly*. For several years from about 1891 he had rooms at 17 Gillingham Street, near Victoria Station.

Even after his marriage there were frequent moves. Like another exile-novelist, Vladimir Nabokov, Conrad never owned a house; and though in Conrad's case the chronic shortage of money must have been a factor, it may also have been that he felt a disinclination to try to send down roots in a country that was not his native land, even though he had become a British subject as early as 1886. In 1896–8 the Conrads lived in the village of Stanford-le-Hope in Essex, some five miles north-east of the port of Tilbury from which Conrad had sailed for the East in his seafaring days, and within a couple of miles of the Thames estuary, on which he sometimes sailed in a boat belonging to his friend Hope, and which is the setting of the opening pages of 'Heart of Darkness'. Their first house in Stanford-le-Hope was small and inconvenient (Conrad called it 'a damned jerry-built rabbit hutch'), and in 1897 they moved to Ivy Walls, an Elizabethan farmhouse on the edge of the village.

In 1898 Conrad moved to Kent, the county on the other side of the Thames estuary; there he was to spend most of the rest of his life, to die, and to be buried. There, too, he formed part of a loosely-knit and somewhat scattered colony of writers. Edward Garnett, Conrad's mentor, lived at Limpsfield, in the neighbouring county of Surrey, from 1896, and Conrad had already visited him there; Ford Madox Hueffer, whom Conrad met through Garnett, lived at Aldington in the 1890s; Stephen Crane lived in Rye in 1899–1900, and Henry James had a house in the same town until his death; and H. G. Wells lived in Folkestone from 1900. It was, therefore, a location that helped to overcome some of the isolation that threatens a writer's life – especially one who, like Conrad, did not care for London and went there as little as possible.

The Conrads' first home in Kent was at Postling, a village three miles north of Hythe, which is one of the ancient Cinque Ports; their home there, Pent Farm, was rented from Hueffer, and it was there that Conrad wrote *Lord Jim*, *Nostromo*, and other books. In 1906–7 they temporarily deserted Kent, spending two long periods in France and Switzerland, and taking up residence in Bedfordshire in September 1907, in a house on the Luton Hoo estate. But in March 1909 they were back in Kent again at Aldington, five miles west of Hythe, in a house, Aldington Knoll, which they borrowed from Hueffer and which boasted a view of Romney Marsh. The following year they moved to Orlestone, five miles south of Ashford; their house, Capel House, was in the Bonnington Road, and there they stayed for nearly a decade. Conrad's last move was to Bishopsbourne, a few miles south-east of Canterbury, where they lived in a Georgian rectory now called Oswalds.

Conrad died there, and after a service in St Thomas's Roman Catholic Church, Canterbury, was buried in Canterbury cemetery. His rather severe, rough-hewn tombstone gives his name as Joseph Teador Conrad Korzeniowski, which, as Frederick R. Karl points out, is neither English nor Polish but an uneasy mixture of the two. It also bears two lines from Spenser's *Faerie Queene*:

> Sleep after toyle, rest after stormie seas,
> Ease after warre, death after life does greatly please.

AFRICA

Marlow's experiences in the Congo recounted in 'Heart of Darkness' closely follow Conrad's own during 1890 (see 'A Conrad Chronology'). Sailing from Bordeaux on 10 May of that year, it took Conrad just over a month to reach Boma, some sixty miles up the Congo. His mood at this time may be gauged from surviving letters: on 15 May, for instance, he wrote to Marguerite Poradowska in a letter evidently mailed from the Canary Islands:

> ... I am comparatively happy, which is all one can hope for here on earth. ... One is sceptical of the future. For indeed, I ask myself, why should anyone have faith in it? And so why be sad? A little illusion, many dreams, a rare flash of happiness; then disillusion, a little anger and much pain, and then the end – peace! That is the programme, and we have to see this tragi-comedy through. We must resign ourselves to it.

On 10 June he wrote to her from Libreville, Gabon:

> After my departure from Boma there may be a long silence. I shall not be able to write until at Leopoldville. It takes twenty days to go there; afoot too! Horrors!

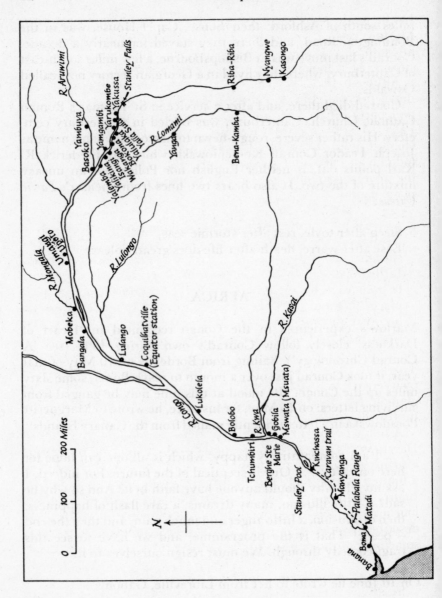

In the story, after spending ten days at the company station, Marlow sets off on a 'two-hundred-mile tramp' and on the fifteenth day reaches Central Station, where repairs to the steamer he is to command take 'some months'.

Although there are some minor adjustments in matters of detail (for example, as Douglas Hewitt points out, the exploration party 'arrived in fact *after* Conrad returned from Stanley Falls'), Marlow's journey into the heart of Africa parallels that of Conrad quite closely in respect of itinerary, timetable, and the individuals encountered on the way. Ian Watt, however, makes the interesting point that Conrad is sparing in his use of actual place-names:

> whereas in 'Youth' nearly all the real place-names are used, in 'Heart of Darkness' only a few unimportant places are specified; as Marlow comments, their names – Gran' Bassam, Little Popo – 'belong to some sordid farce', and they serve only to prepare us for the grotesque world he is entering. For most places Conrad uses general descriptive phrases: Brussels becomes the sepulchral city, Matadi the Company station, and so on; even the Congo is never named, and remains 'that river'.

This generalizing, non-specifying tendency is glossed by Conrad's own remark to Richard Curle that 'explicitness . . . is fatal to the glamour of all artistic work, robbing it of all suggestiveness, destroying all illusion'.

A full account of the interplay of fact and fiction in 'Heart of Darkness' is given in Norman Sherry's *Conrad's Western World*. It is also instructive to read Conrad's 'Congo Diary', first published in a limited edition in 1926 and included in the same year in *Last Essays*, for its graphically detailed account of part of Conrad's journey. The following quotations, from the first of what Curle describes as the 'two small black penny notebooks', suggest something of the nature of the experience:

> [7 July] . . . Walking through long grass for $1\frac{1}{2}$ hours. Crossed a broad river about 100 feet wide and 4 deep . . . walking along an undulating plain towards the Inkandu market on a hill. Hot, thirsty and tired. At 11 arrived on the m[ar]ket place. About 200 people. Business brisk. No water; no camp[in]g place. After remaining for one hour left in search of a resting place. Row

with carriers. No water. At last about 1½ P.M. camped on an
exposed hill side near a muddy creek. No shade. Tent on a
slope. Sun heavy. Wretched. . . . Night miserably cold. No
sleep. Mosquitoes.

Between this uncomfortable siesta and this sleepless night, the
party tramped a distance of 22 miles. Three weeks later Conrad
noted a couple of sights that must have struck his imagination
with the force of symbols:

> [29 July] On the road to-day passed a skeleton tied up to a post.
> Also white man's grave – no name – heap of stones in the form of
> a cross.

Conrad also drew on his African experiences for the story 'An
Outpost of Progress', which may be regarded as an earlier
sketch, in much simpler terms, for 'Heart of Darkness'.

THE EAST

Throughout almost the whole of his writing life, from his first
novel *Almayer's Folly* (1895) to *The Rescue* (1920), Conrad drew
heavily on his own experiences as a merchant seaman in the Far
East, mainly in the region now known as South-East Asia and in
the countries known in Conrad's day as Siam, Malaya, Java,
Sumatra and Borneo. In the 'Author's Note' to *The Shadow-Line* he
speaks of 'that part of the Eastern Seas from which I have carried
away into my writing life the greatest number of suggestions'; and
the parallels between fact and fiction in respect of scenes,
personalities, and even proper names have been shown to be
numerous and close (see, for example, under Ellis, Lingard and
Olmeijer in 'A Conrad Who's Who'). Yet, as Norman Sherry
reminds us, most of Conrad's time in the East was spent not in
'having adventures' (the episodes recounted in 'Youth' and *The
Shadow-Line* being the exceptions that proved the rule) but in the
humdrum routine of a sailor's duties and in periods ashore that
probably were somewhat tedious. Conrad himself tells us in the
'Author's Note' to *Within the Tides* that his life during this period
was 'far from being adventurous in itself' and 'not much charged
with a feeling of romance'. Moreover, most of his time was

inevitably spent in the loneliness of the ocean, and his experiences of life ashore must have been quite limited. For all that, brief glimpses and even second-hand gossip were enough to initiate a process that, years later, produced the novels and stories with an Eastern setting. Perhaps ultimately it matters little whether Conrad actually met the prototype of his Lord Jim (see the entry for Williams in 'A Conrad Who's Who'), or that his contacts with Charles Olmeijer must have been fleeting: there was enough to set his imagination working, and a closer knowledge might have been a handicap rather than an aid to the creative process.

Sherry notes that, as a result of his service on three ships, the *Palestine*, the *Vidar*, and the *Otago*, Conrad became acquainted with 'three strictly limited geographical areas' that feature repeatedly in his fiction – Singapore, Borneo (especially its east coast, in the region of the river Berau), and Bangkok. He first saw Singapore in 1883, after the *Palestine* had been abandoned (see 'Youth'), and it was there that a court of inquiry was held that was later to find a counterpart in *Lord Jim*. The busy port makes an appearance in *The Shadow-Line*, 'The End of the Tether', and elsewhere.

Conrad was back in Singapore in 1885, when it was the destination of his voyage on the *Tilkhurst* (for details of this and other voyages, see 'A Conrad Chronology'), and again in 1887, after he had quitted the *Highland Forest* at Samarang in Java. On this latter occasion he was suffering from a back injury and spent some time in hospital in Singapore. Professor Sherry's researches suggest that the journey from Java to Singapore was made on the *Celestial*, and this name is used for the ship that picks up Marlow at the end of 'Youth'. Subsequently, as mate of the *Vidar*, he saw a good deal of the islands in the South-East Asian archipelago and – most significantly for his later career as a writer – visited Berau and met Charles Olmeijer and Jim Lingard. Sherry comments: 'his contact with the Berau trading post was crucial. From it came *Almayer's Folly*, *An Outcast of the Islands*, the second part of *Lord Jim*, and *The Rescue*'.

Of Conrad's brief visit to Bangkok at the beginning of 1888, Sherry adds that though 'extremely short . . . it was to be almost as fruitful a source for his future fiction as was Berau'. Both *The Shadow-Line* and the remarkable short story 'Falk' draw on the experiences of this time.

Conrad made little use in his fiction of his visits to Australia,

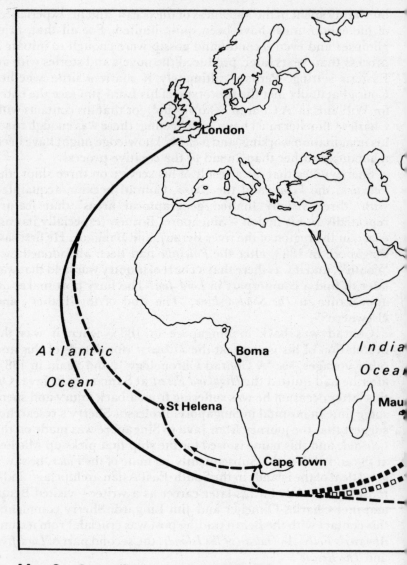

Map 3   *Conrad's sea voyages, 1881–93*

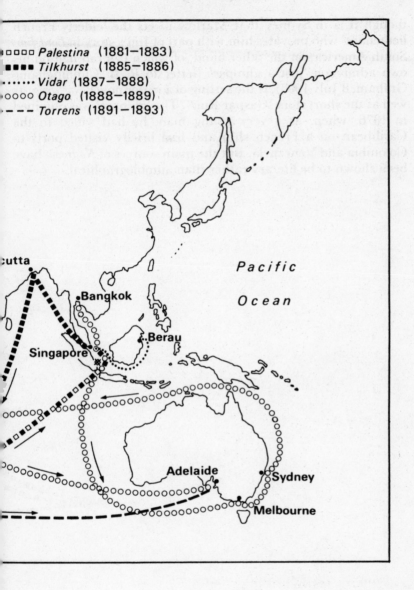

though it is in Sydney that Marlow meets the 'elderly French lieutenant' who provides him with part of Jim's story in *Lord Jim*. South America, on the other hand, of which Conrad had on his own admission 'just a glimpse' (letter to R. B. Cunninghame Graham, 8 July 1903), is the setting of a major novel, *Nostromo*, as well as the short story 'Gaspar Ruiz'. The 'glimpse' was obtained in 1876, when, as a very young man, he had sailed to the Caribbean on a French ship and had briefly visited ports in Colombia and Venezuela. But the main sources of *Nostromo* have been shown to be literary rather than autobiographical.

Conrad Observed

Not surprisingly, most of the accounts of Conrad's appearance, behaviour and speech refer to his later years, after he had settled in England, become a professional writer, and married. Although a few photographs survive from his earlier years, descriptions are scarce. From about the turn of the century, however, they become much more numerous; for while Conrad came to dislike London and did not frequent metropolitan literary coteries, he was not unsociable and enjoyed many friendships, literary and non-literary, as well as welcoming guests into his various homes. Many of those who knew him well, or even slightly, set down their impressions sooner or later – in some cases much later; and in addition we have the testimony of his wife and his two sons. This section quotes briefly from some of the most striking of these accounts in order to present a composite portrait of Conrad the man. Further relevant material will be found in the entries for the following in 'A Conrad Who's Who' above: Epstein, Ford, Galsworthy, Harris, Hope, Morrell, Rothenstein, Russell, Walpole, Wells. Some accounts of Conrad's speech will be found in the next section, 'Conrad's Languages'.

The earliest surviving photograph of Conrad, taken at the age of about five when his family were already in exile, shows a serious, broad-faced child. A photograph of the adolescent Conrad, taken in 1874, the year in which he left Poland for Marseilles, shows him with full lips, dark eyes, and a mane of black hair swept back from his face. Nearly ten years later (1883), in a photograph taken during a visit to Marienbad, he has a moustache and a neatly trimmed beard as well as unusually full eyebrows. Most of the photographs from his later years show Conrad with friends or members of his family; and some of the

49

best of them, like those already mentioned, are included in Najder's biography. There are also good selections of photographs in Karl's biography and in Norman Sherry's *Conrad and his World* (1973).

A late photograph, taken in 1923, shows Conrad formally attired and still unmistakably foreign in appearance; and in the year of his death his portrait was painted by Walter Tittle (now in the National Portrait Gallery; see Plate 5a). Only a few weeks before he died, Conrad sat for a bust by Jacob Epstein which Najder describes as 'Conrad's most impressive portrait'.

Verbal descriptions of Conrad begin with what is presumably a self-description, on the application form for the examination to qualify as a master in 1886, where the entry under 'personal description' refers to dark complexion, dark hair, and hazel eyes. These details, as Najder points out, are confirmed from other sources – which is more than can be said of the statement that his height was 5 feet 9½ inches. At that time such a height would have been somewhat above average; but Conrad struck his contemporaries as being rather on the short side – Edward Garnett says he was 'short', and among other descriptions are those of H. G. Wells ('rather short'), H.-D. Davray ('slightly less than average in height'), Ford Madox Ford ('small'), and Paul Langlois ('slightly below average'). It looks remarkably as though, even on the official form, Conrad was recording a wish rather than a fact – a not uncommon habit with him.

Paul Langlois, who encountered Conrad in Port Louis, Mauritius, in 1888, provides one of the fullest of the earlier accounts, though it needs to be borne in mind that he set down his impressions more than forty years after the event. Langlois recalled Conrad's 'forceful and very mobile features' and his 'distinguished manners': 'always dressed like a dandy', he was not, it seems, popular with his fellow-sailors, who ironically dubbed him 'the Russian Count' (a label that is not likely to have endeared them to Conrad, who detested the Russians). Langlois also notes his 'very varied and interesting conversation' and the fluency and elegance of his French.

Six years later, on 8 October 1894, Edward Garnett met Conrad for the first time in the London office of the publisher T. Fisher Unwin, and later recalled 'a dark-haired man, short but extremely graceful in his nervous gestures, with brilliant eyes' and a manner of speech that was 'ingratiating, guarded, and brusque turn by turn'. Garnett also mentions Conrad's extreme politeness, and this quality was to strike a number of observers even in a period when manners were habitually more formal than they are nowadays. Garnett, again, wrote that 'Conrad's courtesy was part of his being, bred in the bone'; E. V. Lucas, the critic and essayist, said he had 'manners so punctilious that they made one's own seem almost to be rudeness'; Ernest Dawson described his manners as 'courtly'; William Rothenstein described him as 'extremely courteous . . . by nature', and referred to his 'gallantry' and 'chivalry' (uncommon words to use even two or three generations ago); and Desmond MacCarthy, who did not meet Conrad until 1922, found him 'somewhat elaborate in courtesies. . . . He had the kind of manners which improve those of a visitor beyond recognition'.

It seems clear that this is an aspect of Conrad's behaviour that was not diminished even by long residence in England; and for MacCarthy as for others it was part of his unmistakable foreignness ('He was very much the *foreign* gentleman' – a phrase in which the stress falls on the noun as well as the adjective). In 1912, an American visitor, J. G. Huneker, found in Conrad a man 'whose ways were French, Polish, anything but "literary", bluff, or English'; and a little later Jane Anderson judged 'all that he did, all that he said, inexplicably alien to England. It was not that he was foreign; it was simply that he was not English'. To the end Conrad spoke English with a strong accent, and his pronunciation was evidently a factor in these judgments. But there was also an unEnglish quality in his elaborate and courtly gestures: Jane Anderson, again, recalled him 'talking very fast and making tremendous motions with his hands and his shoulders'. Ford had earlier noted that 'He gesticulated with his hands and shoulders when he wished to be emphatic, but when he forgot himself in the excitement of talking he gesticulated with his whole body, throwing himself about in his chair'; and Wells also described 'the gestures of his hands and arms' as 'from the shoulders and very Oriental indeed'. The carefully trimmed beard and the monocle that Conrad sometimes wore no doubt also contributed to this impression.

'Oriental' is an epithet used by another observer, Sir Henry Newbolt, but this time in reference to Conrad's face. Archibald Marshall found his head 'magnificent' and his whole figure 'unforgettable'. Edwin Pugh's vivid account of his first impressions of Conrad describe his appearance as 'simian': 'His head was a little askew and seemed somehow to be unduly sunken between his unusually high shoulders. His forehead, which was of a cold, shining whiteness, receded sharply from his heavy brows'. Though unflattering, this account is borne out by many of the photographs and portraits. Desmond MacCarthy describes the head and face in more detail:

> The length of his head from chin to crown struck me, and this was accentuated by a pointed greyish beard, which a backward carriage of his head on high shoulders projected forwards. Black eyebrows, hooked nose, hunched shoulders, gave him a more hawk-like look than even his photograph had suggested.

The striking quality of Conrad's eyes was often a matter for comment. The early account by Paul Langlois mentions 'big black eyes usually melancholy and dreamy, and gentle as well, except for fairly frequent moments of irritation'. Garnett refers to 'brilliant eyes, now narrowed and penetrating, now soft and warm'. Later in Conrad's life, Jane Anderson found in his eyes 'a curious hypnotic quality'; Cecil Roberts noted that they were 'slant lidded' and 'brightened like the eyes of a bird when he looked at you'; and Jean-Aubry writes that 'Under his drooping eyelids which at times made him look drowsy or day-dreaming, his eyes retained such a piercing expression that one could not doubt their constant alertness'. Both Galsworthy and Rothenstein also described the eyes as 'piercing', and Sir Christopher Cockerell found that they 'looked out almost fiercely'.

Many accounts bear witness to Conrad's scrupulous neatness and even elegance of dress. Cockerell, for instance, found him 'extremely well dressed, with a perfectly trimmed beard and an elegant beautiful figure' – this more than thirty years after Langlois had described Conrad as a dandy. There seems to have been some difference of opinion on the question whether his appearance betrayed signs of his years of seafaring. Ernest Dawson met him at the beginning of the century and long afterwards recalled Conrad wearing 'a peaked cap of maritime cut, which, with his jacket and trousers of stout blue cloth, gave him somewhat of the aspect of a pilot'. Rothenstein, who met Conrad not long afterwards, remarked that 'in some ways he looked like the sea captain, but his nervous manner, his rapid, excited speech, his restlessness, his high shoulders, did not suggest the sailor,' and added that 'I accepted him at once as an artist'. Meeting Conrad towards the end of his life, Mrs Kate Meyrick, the owner of a West End nightclub frequented by Conrad, judged him 'exactly what he was – an ex-sailor', with his 'short rough beard' and 'clothes of nautical cut'. Bertrand Russell, on the other hand, found that 'nothing in his demeanour in any way suggested the sea. He was an aristocratic Polish gentleman to his fingertips'. In considering many of these accounts, due allowance must be made for the fallibility of memory; and in any case it may be that some observers, knowing of Conrad's first career, saw what they expected to see.

This section may conclude with a few passages not given elsewhere in this volume that recall life with Conrad. In the chapter titled 'Working with Conrad' in his volume of memoirs *Return to Yesterday* (1932), Ford Madox Ford draws a vivid picture of their collaboration over *Romance* – a picture that conveys something of Conrad's volatile, not to say manic-depressive, temperament:

> And it was astonishing what small things could call down to his underlying buoyancy. I remember once we had been struggling with *Romance* for hours and hours, and he had been in complete despair, and everything that I had suggested had called forth his bitterest gibes, and he was sick, and over ears in debt, and penniless. And we had come to a blank full-stop – one of those intervals when the soul *must* pause to breathe, and love itself have rest. And Mrs. Conrad came in and said that the mare had trotted from Postling Vents to Sandling in five minutes – say, twelve miles an hour! At once, there in the room was Conrad-Jack-ashore! The world was splendid; hope nodded from every rosebud that looked over the window-sill of the low room. We were going to get a car and go to Canterbury; the mare should have a brand new breeching strap. And in an incredibly short space of time – say, three hours – at least half a page of *Romance* got itself written.
>
> That was how it went, day in day out, for years – the despair, the lamentations continuing for hours, and then the sudden desperate attack on the work – the attack that would become the fabulous engrossment. We would write for whole days, for half nights, for half the day, or all the night. We would jot down

passages on scraps of paper or on the margins of books, handing them one to the other or exchanging them. We would roar with laughter over passages that would have struck no other soul as humorous; Conrad would howl with rage and I would almost sigh over others that no other soul perhaps would have found as bad as we considered them. We would recoil one from the other and go each to our own cottage – our cottages at that period never being further the one from the other than an old mare could take us in an afternoon. In those cottages we would prepare other drafts and so drive backwards and forwards with packages of manuscript under the dog-cart seats. . . . (p. 197)

But the stresses and strains of authorship were not, of course, the whole of Conrad's life; and for a portrait of him in more relaxed mood we may turn to the autobiography of David Garnett (son of Edward), *Golden Echo* (1953):

Joseph Conrad paid many visits to the Cearne [the Garnetts' Surrey home). On one of the first occasions, when I was five years old, I asked him why the first mate of a ship was always a bad man and the second mate good. I don't know what stories I had been reading which had put this into my head, but I remember Conrad's laughing and confusing me by saying: "For many years I was a first mate myself."

It was next morning that we made friends. There was a jolly wind, and it was washing-day. I was alone with Conrad, and suddenly he was making me a sailing boat. The sail was a clean sheet tied at the top corners to a clothes-prop and hoisted with some spare clothes-line over one of the clothes-posts. The sail was lashed at the foot, and I held the sheet fastened to the other corner in one hand while it bellied and pulled. The green grass heaved in waves, the sail filled and tugged, our speed was terrific. Alterations were made and the rig perfected and when, an hour later, Edward came out looking for his guest, he found him sitting in our big clothes basket steering the boat and giving me orders to take in or let out the sail. (p. 62)

In his *Joseph Conrad: Times Remembered* (1981), Conrad's younger son John gives a somewhat similar but fuller account of Conrad the novelist relaxing for long enough to play the game of being Conrad the mariner once again:

I had been given a yawl-rigged model yacht. . . . It was a most precious possession and I was only allowed to sail it when either JC or my brother could accompany me to the pond. Some days passed before we tried her out since long and animated discussions took place to decide on a suitable name for her. It was finally settled by my father that she should be called the *Narcissus* and she was named and launched from the new slipway at Bangkok which JC had helped me to build.

The moat was too weedy and the 'Round' pond near the north end was too small so we took her to a long but narrow sheet of water not quite half a mile away in the field opposite the 'Sugarloaf' cottage. It was about two hundred and twenty feet long by some thirty feet wide, with a spinney along the south side and a medium-sized oak tree stood on the edge of the high vertical bank at the eastern end where the water was quite deep. At the opposite end it was shallow for about four or five feet from the edge and JC always appointed me 'harbour master' here before taking up his position at the other end. On this particular day there was not a lot of wind and what there was was flukey but the *Narcissus* came steadily towards me. I caught her at the water's edge, turned her round, reset the sails and gave her a gentle push back to JC waiting at the other end. The wind dropped to the merest puff and the *Narcissus* barely moved but eventually she drew near the eastern end but then 'hove to' just out of JC's reach. After waiting a short while he hooked the walking stick he was carrying over a bough of the oak tree without realising it was rotten, and leant out over the water to grab the top of the mainmast. He had just reached it when, with a loud crack, the bough broke and JC fell into the deep end with a great splash. As the waves subsided I saw him slowly floundering towards the bank and rushed round to give him a hand as the water was over his shoulders. After much puffing and blowing he managed to get out and stand up with the water pouring from his clothes. I was much too concerned to laugh, which was as well, as he was very angry. He told me to pick up the yacht and we set off for home with JC muttering under his breath 'damned circus – blasted tree – fool enterprise'. By the time we reached the road he was in a better frame of mind and as we walked homewards he said,

'What an affair! I've been aloft furling the main tops'l in a full gale and survived and now to be nearly drowned in a muddy

English pond would have been too bad but Fate relented. Keep all this to yourself. – Just say I slipped!' (pp. 28–9)

Conrad's other son, Borys, also published a volume of reminiscences of his father, *My Father: Joseph Conrad* (1970), from which the following passage is taken as evidence that, at any rate in the more affluent circumstances of his later years, Conrad could be a genial host – a social role to be set against the more familiar picture of his agonies at his desk:

> J.C. was an excellent host and he greatly enjoyed giving Sunday luncheon parties, at which he was always in great form. Intimate friends were invited for the weekend within the limits of the accommodation available, and others travelled from London to Canterbury on Sunday morning by train and were met at the station by our car. There would sometimes be eight or ten guests at the luncheon table, some of them Polish or French, and I was always fascinated by J.C.'s ability to carry on a brilliant conversation in three languages without interfering with his enjoyment of the meal, and still find time to 'damn' his manservant – who acted as butler on these occasions – for some real or imagined defect in the service. Angela and Carola Zagorska, J.C.'s cousins and nearest Polish relatives, spent a good deal of time at Oswalds during this period and were often present at these Sunday luncheons. Yes, J.C. really enjoyed entertaining his friends and they were equally happy in his company. In Curle's words: 'The position of host at the head of his table before a large and kindred gathering, and the position of a friend in a tête-à-tête conversation late at night in front of a dwindling fire saw Conrad at his best.' (p. 154)

As Borys Conrad also recounts, his father was less genial under the social stresses of another occasion:

> One event which remains very clear in my memory is the occasion of H. G. Wells' first visit to luncheon, a meal over which my Mother, who always coped personally with all culinary matters, had taken particular pains. To begin with H.G. arrived half-an-hour late. This fact, in itself, was sufficient to ruffle my Father's temper and disrupt my Mother's preparations for the repast, but it faded into insignificance when H.G.

took his place at the table and announced his wish to lunch off a glass of milk and two aspirins from his waistcoat pocket. So far as I recollect, my Mother's self-control was quite admirable, but my Father, having first screwed his monocle firmly in position, treated the guest to a most virulent glare. I have no further recollection of this visit but it must have ended upon a friendly note because we went to the Wells' home, Spade House, upon several subsequent occasions. . . . (p. 30)

Conrad's wife Jessie may be allowed to have the last word. Jessie Conrad has often been maligned, sometimes for reasons of envy or snobbery that are only too apparent. It is true that as a chronicler she suffers from the unreliability that seems to have been infectious in the Conrad circle; and her enemies sometimes said that her versions of anecdotes tended to redound to her own credit. Be that as it may, there is no doubt that she put up gallantly with the moods of a man who must often have been almost impossible to live with; though often in severe pain herself, she nursed him devotedly through his illnesses, and enjoyed a relationship that seems to have been happy and relaxed, despite (or because of) the profound differences between the couple. In her *Joseph Conrad as I Knew Him* (1926), she gives a good-humoured account of the combination of eloquence and cavalier disregard for fact that characterized Conrad as a talker:

. . . Conrad had far too lively an imagination for everyday events. He lived life as a novel; he exaggerated simple trifles, though quite unconsciously. But his imagination made him a wonderful talker. I have been amazed sometimes while hearing him talk and hold a whole roomful spellbound. In those days, before his voice became uncertain, before he grew to distrust it and in consequence to strain it till it was sometimes painful to listen to him, he would start off, spurred by some remark, and recall some long-forgotten incident out of the depths of his memory. He would pace the room, gesticulating in his usual picturesque manner, and his hearers would be very attentive and for the most part silent. But now and then perhaps some one would interrupt with a question; this temerity usually called forth a more emphatic statement and still more energetic movements of the hands. Often and often I have sat and marvelled at the extent to which, in his mouth, the same story varied. Each statement, if the same in the main, would be entirely different in detail . . .

Conrad had one very marked characteristic: he would allow no argument in his own family circle. In early days I often transgressed by attempting to correct his dates. I have heard him repeatedly give the date of our marriage as two years later than it was. At first I interrupted him eagerly, pointing out that our boy was born that year. He would turn quickly towards me, frowning his displeasure: "You will allow me, my dear, to know as much about it as you do. After all, he is my son as well as yours – besides, I never consider you as old as that." Though this was not a very cogent argument, I had perforce to hold my tongue . . . (pp. 16–18)

Among many other anecdotes, Jessie Conrad gives in the same book these examples of Conrad's blend of impatience and absent-mindedness which, if not necessarily authentic, are certainly *ben trovato*:

Once, when we were in town together, I was told off to secure rooms in the hotel where we usually stayed. Conrad, as he had some business, arranged to join me later. (I remember vividly his comic disgust while relating what had happened to him, in the interval.) His business over, he had walked rapidly into another hotel and curtly requested the waiter to "tell my wife I am here." The waiter's very natural question, "What name, sir?" had exasperated him, and he had answered sharply, "Mrs. Conrad, of course." When the man returned after a short absence with the information that there was no one of that name in the hotel, Conrad called for the manager, and now, greatly irate, turned on him tensely with the command, "Produce my wife!" It was with difficulty he was persuaded that he was in the wrong hotel. (p. 22)

Our boy Borys was born in January 1898, on a mild and bright forenoon, while Conrad (so I have been told) was wandering vaguely among the beds of the kitchen garden. Suddenly he heard a child cry, and approaching the house where Rose, the maid we had then, was at work – "Send that child away at once; it will disturb Mrs. Conrad!" he shouted.

"It's your own child, sir," the girl answered indignantly.

Just then my mother ran downstairs to give him a few details, "Such a big boy," and ran back indoors. Whatever his feelings might have been, he managed to conceal them beneath an air of detached interest. (p. 43)

Recollections of Conrad will be found in the following sources among others:

David Bone, 'Memories of Conrad', *Saturday Review of Literature*, 7 November 1925. (Bone, a sailor, met Conrad in Liverpool at the end of 1919 and was captain of the *Tuscania*, on which Conrad later sailed to New York.)

Cyril Clemens, 'A Chat with Joseph Conrad', *Conradiana*, II (1969–70).

Ernest Dawson, 'Some Recollections of Joseph Conrad', *Fortnightly Review*, 1 August 1928. (Dawson met Conrad at the home of H. G. Wells in about 1902.)

Norman Douglas, *Looking Back* (1931).

Robin Douglas, 'My Boyhood with Conrad', *Cornhill Magazine*, I (1929).

J. G. Huneker, *Steeplejack* (New York, 1920). (Huneker was an American author and critic who visited Conrad in 1912.)

E. V. Lucas, *Reading, Writing, and Remembering* (1932). (Lucas was an English essayist and critic introduced to Conrad by Edward Garnett in the mid-nineties.)

Desmond MacCarthy, *Portraits* (1931). (MacCarthy, reviewer and man of letters, visited Conrad in 1922.)

H. V. Marrot, *Life and Letters of John Galsworthy* (1935).

Archibald Marshall, *Out and About* (1934). (Marshall was a journalist and editor who met Conrad in 1907.)

Henry Newbolt, *My World as in my Time* (1932). (A once-popular poet, Newbolt met Conrad in 1905.)

Edwin Pugh, 'Joseph Conrad as I Knew Him', *T.P.'s and Cassell's Weekly*, 23 August 1924. (Pugh, journalist and author, met Conrad in about 1899.)

Ernest Rhys, 'An Interview with Joseph Conrad', *Bookman*, December 1922.

Cecil Roberts, *Half Way* (1931). (Roberts met Conrad in about 1917.)

J. G. Sutherland, *At Sea with Joseph Conrad* (Boston, 1922).

(Sutherland was captain of the *Ready*, on which Conrad sailed in 1916.)

Walter Tittle, 'Portraits in Pencil and Pen: III. Joseph Conrad', *Strand Magazine*, June 1924. (Tittle painted Conrad's portrait towards the end of his life.)

Paul Valéry, 'Sujet d'une conversation avec Conrad', *Nouvelle Revue Française*, XII (1924). (The French poet met Conrad in London in 1922, and subsequently visited him at his home.)

H. F. West, 'Joseph Conrad's Funeral', *Saturday Review of Literature*, 6 September 1924.

Other sources are cited under the appropriate entries in 'A Conrad Who's Who'. There is a useful short survey of relevant material, with some further references, in Norman Sherry's *Conrad: The Critical Heritage*, pp. 38–9.

Conrad's Languages

... when one considers his personal history, the English of his books is something like a miracle (George Gissing to Edward Clodd, 30 November 1902).

I've been so cried up of late as a sort of freak, an amazing bloody foreigner writing in English ... (Conrad to Edward Garnett, 4 October 1907).

Conrad's mother tongue was, of course, Polish; but towards the end of his life, and after long residence in England, married to an English wife, and with largely English-speaking friends, his Polish seems to have deteriorated. Najder points out that, in commenting on an indifferent Polish translation of his story 'Il Conde', Conrad showed a sense of Polish style that was 'in general uneven and incomplete'. He adds that Conrad's few letters in Polish from his later years show a deterioration of syntactical control, and that 'whenever he wanted to express a more complex idea, he resorted to French expressions'.

According to his wife Jessie, whenever Conrad was seriously ill and in a state of delirium he would 'rave in Polish' (*Joseph Conrad and his Contemporaries*, p. 26). This occurred, for instance, during his grave illness just after the completion of *Under Western Eyes*. In the light of this fact, the powerful short story 'Amy Foster' – which H. G. Wells perceptively described as both 'an amazingly good story' and 'a sort of caricature autobiography' – seems to contain an undeniable personal element.

Conrad was thoroughly at home in French, which he had learned in childhood (he had also learned a certain amount of Latin, Greek, and German, but in French had attained a degree of fluency).* His period of residence in Switzerland in 1873, and still more his time in Marseilles (from the autumn of 1874 to the spring of 1878, with interruptions) and his periods spent on French ships, would have increased his fluency; and Paul Langlois (see p. 50 above) recalled that he spoke French 'with elegance'. There are also other accounts that testify to the excellence of his French accent. H.-D. Davray, for instance, who translated some of Conrad's work into French, noted that he spoke the language 'with great ease and no trace of an accent'. According to Ford Madox Ford, he and Conrad conversed habitually in French, with Conrad occasionally observing that 'There's a word *so-and-so* in Polish to express what I want' (*Joseph Conrad: A Personal Remembrance*, p. 158). Ford also states that Conrad told him:

> I write with much difficulty; my intimate, automatic, less expressed thoughts are in Polish; when I express myself with care I do it in French. When I write I think in French and then translate the words of my thoughts into English

but like many of Ford's statements this needs to be viewed with some scepticism.

Although Conrad's father translated Dickens and Shakespeare, and Conrad himself read these authors in Polish during his early years, he seems to have known nothing of the English language until he began to serve on British ships. According to his own account, he heard his first words of English on board the *Mavis*, the steamer on which he sailed to the eastern Mediterranean in 1878. (There is perhaps some slight and pardonable hyperbole in this account, since it is hard to believe that he would not at least have overheard, and perhaps have met, English visitors to France during his residence there.) He told Cunninghame Graham (letter of 4 February 1898) that he 'began to learn English' while serving on the *Skimmer of the Sea* between Lowestoft and Newcastle later in 1898, his mentors being 'East Coast chaps each built as

---

* In his *Multilingualism* (Leyden, 1963), Veroboj Vildomec cites Conrad as an instance of 'really remarkable, and possibly unique, achievement among multilinguals' and treats him as quadrilingual. However, there seems to be no evidence that Conrad knew sufficient German for it to be ranked with Polish, French and English. Vildomec's suggestions that at one period of his life Conrad 'seems to have developed a kind of alien complex which is typical of some foreigners who have to live and earn their living among the English' (p. 57) and that 'his multilingualism was probably a factor in the slowness of his work' (p. 58) carry more conviction.

though to last for ever, and coloured like a Christmas card'. He evidently made good progress, for two years later, when he sat for the examination to qualify as second mate, he was required (as Najder points out) to prove 'to the satisfaction of the Examiners' that he could 'speak and write the English language sufficiently well to perform the duties required . . . on board a British vessel'; and this he did successfully.

To the end of his life Conrad's English accent, unlike his French, remained unmistakably foreign: Paul Valéry, indeed, who met Conrad in 1923, described it as 'horrible', and commented: 'To be a great writer in a language which one speaks so badly is a rare and eminently original thing.' Edward Garnett makes the interesting point that Conrad had acquired much of his English, and especially the more literary elements in his vocabulary, through reading rather than conversation; and as a result,

when he read aloud to me some new written MS pages [of *An Outcast of the Islands*] . . . he mispronounced so many words that I followed him with difficulty. I found then that he had never once heard these English words spoken, but had learned them all from books!

According to Ford, Conrad

spoke English with great fluency and distinction, with correctitude in his syntax, his words absolutely exact as to meaning but his accentuation so faulty that he was at times difficult to understand and his use of adverbs as often as not eccentric.

Wells makes a similar point:

He had learnt to read English long before he spoke it and he had formed wrong sound impressions of many familiar words; he had for example acquired an incurable tendency to pronounce the last *e* in these and those.

Wells also notes that 'When he talked of seafaring his terminology was excellent but when he turned to less familiar topics he was often at a loss for phrases'. Just as Ford had observed that, when speaking French, Conrad would resort to Polish if stuck for the word he needed, Wells comments that in speaking English he 'would supplement his vocabulary – especially if he were discussing cultural or political matters – with French words'. Najder argues that Conrad agreed to collaborate with Ford in order to improve his English: 'Until then the two principal sources of Conrad's knowledge of English were the colloquial language of the sailors and the books he read; that left substantial areas where he was insecure.'

There are numerous accounts of the way in which Conrad's spoken English struck those who met him. Ernest Dawson wrote that 'he could not utter two words in English without betraying that it was not his mother tongue'; Bertrand Russell noted that he 'spoke English with a very strong foreign accent'; and Jane Anderson detected 'an accent which I have never heard before. It is an accent which affects every word, and gives the most extraordinary rhythm to phrases. And his verbs are never right'. Lady Ottoline Morrell recalled that

> He talked English with a strong accent, as if he tasted his words in his mouth before pronouncing them; but he talked extremely well, though he had always the talk and manner of a foreigner.

There is evidence that Conrad himself was somewhat self-conscious about his command of spoken English. When he was invited to give public readings from his work, he told Elbridge L. Adams that he was 'not very anxious to display my accent before a large gathering of people. It might affect them disagreeably' (letter of 20 November 1922). When he was at last prevailed upon to read extracts from *Victory* to a specially invited audience during his visit to America, one of the audience recalled that 'his pronunciation was so bad. . . . Conrad spoke English with a guttural Polish twist'. Cunninghame Graham's impression was that Conrad's foreign accent in speaking English became more, not less, evident as he grew older; and certainly Virginia Woolf depicted him in her diary on 23 June 1920 as 'a foreigner, talking broken English'.

For all the range of vocabulary and sense of the expressiveness of English words that he eventually acquired, Conrad's hold on his adopted language could be precarious, and he makes occasional errors of grammar or usage even in his later works. There is frequent evidence of 'interference' in his English style by Polish or French. Ian Watt, in his *Conrad in the Nineteenth Century* (p. 296), notes that the influence of Polish can be seen in the opening sentence of *Lord Jim*, where, in the phrase 'he advanced straight at you . . . , a plural action is given a highly specific and dramatic quality'. Watt writes:

> English has no special form of the verb for habitual, consuetudinal, iterative, or frequentative usages; instead, it relies on modal auxiliaries, as in Conrad's 'Perhaps it would be'. Conrad was no doubt influenced by Polish, which, unlike Latin and the Germanic languages, has a fully developed plural aspect for verbs, and there may have been a residue of this in Conrad's habitual and 'slightly unusual use of the word "would" ' on which Ford commented . . .

On the influence of Polish on Conrad's English style, see I. P. Pulc, 'The Imprint of Polish on Conrad's Prose', in *Joseph Conrad: Theory and World Fiction* (Lubbock, Texas, 1974).

For obvious reasons, the influence of French has been more widely commented on. An anonymous reviewer of *The Nigger of the 'Narcissus'* in the *Glasgow Herald* (9 December 1897) noted that 'Mr Conrad . . . betrays an occasional fondness for the use of most unusual words', and, quoting a couple of sentences from that story ('French nails polished and slim. They lay in a solid mass more *inabordable* than a hedgehog'), enquired: 'Is this a result of the wide circulation of Dr Murray's Oxford Dictionary?' The answer is, of course, no: it is an example – one among many – of Conrad's use of a common French word as if it were an acceptable English one. In his *Joseph Conrad* (1968), J. I. M. Stewart cites some other examples:

> In *Nostromo* there is the celebrated case of the three horsemen 'arrested' in the course of a journey, where all that is intended is that they have come to a halt. In *Lord Jim* we read that 'Rajah Allang pretended to be the only trader in his country' [recalling *prétendre*, to claim, rather than the normal English meaning of the verb]; in *The Secret Agent* a woman has 'no conscience of how little she had audibly said' . . . and a composer is 'in pass of becoming famous' . . . ; in 'Amy Foster' there is a room 'taken upon the space of that sort of coach-house'.

Richard Curle pointed out a gallicism in Conrad's *Congo Diary*,

where a track through the jungle is described as 'accidented'.
(Baines, however, reminds us that it is significant that Conrad
should have chosen to write his private diary in English.)

To these minor quirks of diction we must add the occasional
influence of French syntax, observable, for instance, in Conrad's
placing of the adverb and in his fondness for the unEnglish
pattern of a noun followed by two adjectives. All this suggests
that, when he 'adopted' English, Conrad did not altogether desert
French, into which he often slips in his letters. It is surely
revealing that, when he spent some time in France and was
engaged in revising the French translations of some of his stories,
he wrote: 'Work at a standstill . . . my English has all departed
from me' (letter of 8 January 1907). At about the same time, he
told Marguerite Poradowska that 'English is for me still a foreign
language and its use requires a formidable effort on my part' – this
after the completion of *Lord Jim*, *Nostromo*, and indeed the greater
part of his best work. In the following year he compared himself to
'a coal-miner in his pit quarrying all my English sentences out of
a black night' (to Garnett, 28 August 1908), and the effort of
writing in a language that was not his mother tongue must have
contributed to the anguish that Conrad so often experienced
during composition.

Three weeks before the letter just quoted, Robert Lynd,
reviewing *A Set of Six* in the *Daily News* (6 August 1908), had
referred to Conrad as a man 'without either country or language'
who 'writes in English by choice, as it were, rather than by
nature'. These remarks touched Conrad on a very sensitive spot,
and Najder persuasively suggests that they stimulated him not
long afterwards to begin work on *A Personal Record*, which contains
a large element of self-justification. It is there, for instance, that he
speaks of himself as having been 'adopted by the genius of the
language', refers to English as 'the speech of my secret choice',
and claims that 'if I had not written in English I would not have
written at all'.

Conrad makes a similar point in a letter to Hugh Walpole dated
7 June 1918. In his book on Conrad published two years earlier,
Walpole promulgated the story that, before embarking on his
career as an author, Conrad had hesitated between French and
English as his medium. Conrad protested:

It is absurd. When I wrote the first words of *A F* [*Almayer's Folly*]

I had been already for years and years *thinking* in English. I began to think in English long before I mastered, I won't say the style (I haven't done that yet), but the mere uttered speech. . . . You may take it from me that if I had not known English I wouldn't have written a line for print in my life.

The same letter adds that he 'would have been afraid to grapple with French', which is as a literary language 'more exacting and less appealing'; 'But there was never any alternative offered or even dreamed of.' Like his similar claim that he would never have become a writer if he had not met the prototype of 'Almayer', this need not be taken entirely at face value: for one thing, Najder points out that 'the possibility of writing in French had been mentioned several times in Conrad's earlier letters and projects'. The notion of his becoming an *English* writer – like that of his becoming, as he puts it (again in *A Personal Record*), 'a British seaman and no other' – seems to have been largely a product of Conrad's inveterate self-mythologizing; and, although Najder remarks somewhat severely that he 'tried to cover up his tracks', it may have been mainly unconscious. That Conrad to the end felt himself to be in a real sense an alien, and felt it deeply, is suggested by the reason he gave for saying that he would not be an appropriate recipient for the Order of Merit, the highest public honour that can be bestowed on an English author: that he was one 'who, whatever my deepest feelings may be, can't claim English literature as my inheritance' (letter of 15 February 1919). Najder's summing-up carries conviction:

. . . Conrad wished to infuse his life, and particularly the public aspect of it that he regarded as most precious – his works of fiction – with the sense of an overriding purposefulness; he did not want the tricky problem of language ('tricky' for the English because of the occasionally questioned correctness of Conrad's language, and for Poles because of 'patriotic' concerns) to appear to have been determined by external circumstances. (pp. 115–16)

The Novels

ALMAYER'S FOLLY

'I am not a facile inventor', wrote Conrad in a letter of 24 May 1912; and he makes the same point in the Author's Note to *Tales of Unrest*, where he declares that 'The sustained invention of a really telling lie demands a talent which I do not possess.' Conrad's fiction, especially his earlier fiction, draws heavily on personal experience: not only settings but characters are often based on actuality, and he even goes so far as to retain the names of his real-life prototypes or close approximations to them. The experience, it needs to be added, was filtered through memory, since his two careers – as sailor and novelist, widely-travelled man of action and sedentary professional author – were not concurrent but consecutive. He spent most of the period 1883–8 in the Far East, and he uses Eastern settings in his work from *Almayer's Folly* (1895) to *The Rescue* (1920).

However, as Norman Sherry points out in *Conrad's Eastern World*, he spent only a few months ashore during this period and 'primarily he must have been limited to sea-going society and mariners' talk both on the sea and ashore'. Conrad himself wrote to J. M. Dent on 27 March 1917: 'But indeed I knew very little of and about shore people', and he complained to Edward Garnett on one occasion that 'I know nothing, nothing! except from the outside. I have to guess at everything!' It will not do, therefore, to exaggerate the extent to which a novel such as *Almayer's Folly* is a mere transcription of experience; and while it owes much to first-hand observation, it also shows the strong influence of literary models.

In 1887, during a voyage to Java, Conrad had received a back

68

injury from a falling spar, and on reaching Singapore he went into hospital for treatment. On leaving hospital, he signed on (August) as chief mate of the steamship *Vidar* under Captain Craig, and remained with the ship until the beginning of 1888. It was during this period that he made several journeys in local waters and met Charles Olmeijer, the prototype of Almayer. (In the novel his first name is changed to Kaspar and the spelling of the surname is Anglicized.) When the *Vidar* made a stop some thirty miles up the Berau river in Eastern Borneo, Conrad encountered Olmeijer, who had been living there for about seventeen years and was acting as a representative of Captain William Lingard (Tom Lingard in the novel), a trader and adventurer well-known in the area. Later, in *A Personal Record*, Conrad gave an account of their first meeting, and the two men seem to have met on a few subsequent occasions, though in the circumstances none of Conrad's visits to the settlement can have lasted more than a very short time.,

As Ian Watt notes in his excellent account of the origins of this novel (*Conrad in the Nineteenth Century*, ch. 2), in accounting for the presence of Olmeijer/Almayer in this remote spot Conrad 'keeps fairly close to the historical facts' – for example, the real Lingard and Olmeijer did prospect for gold and deal in contraband arms and gunpowder – but he also makes some significant changes. Olmeijer had the company of three other white men at Berau, but Conrad stresses Almayer's isolation by making him (in the words of the ironic epitaph on the novel's last page) 'the only man on the east coast [of Borneo]'. Olmeijer had four surviving children, but Almayer has only one. Olmeijer was a half-caste; Almayer is of Dutch parentage on both sides, though he was born in the East and, importantly, has never seen the Europe he dreams of.

In *A Personal Record* Conrad recounts how, one morning in 1889, while living in lodgings in London, he sat down and began to write: the impulse, according to his own account, was an obscure and half-realized one, but he adds that 'it is possible and even likely that I was thinking of the man Almayer'. Though 'begun in idleness', the novel occupied him for five years, during which (according to one of Conrad's letters) 'there was not a day I did not think of it'. A draft was completed in April 1894, and a typescript was submitted to a publisher (Fisher Unwin) on 4 July of that year. It was accepted in October on the advice of their reader, Edward Garnett, and the novel was published on 29 April

1895, in an edition of 2000 copies, the author's name appearing on the title-page as Joseph Conrad.

On both sides of the Atlantic it received favourable reviews. For most contemporary critics *Almayer's Folly* was, in the words of a reviewer in the *London Mercury* a quarter-century later, 'an immense and exhilarating surprise' in that it boldly opened up new fictional territory. Arthur Waugh noted in the *Critic* (May 1895) that Borneo, 'a tract hitherto untouched by the novelist', was now 'annexed by Mr Joseph Conrad, a new writer'; the *Spectator* critic (October 1895) hoped that Conrad might become 'the Kipling of the Malay Archipelago' (a remark that incidentally draws attention to Conrad's late start as a writer, since he was eight years older than Kipling); and the *Saturday Review* critic, probably H. G. Wells, ventured to predict (June 1895) that the novel would secure its author 'a high place among contemporary story-tellers'. As Norman Sherry points out in *Conrad: The Critical Heritage*, 'Conrad's impact was distinct and forceful', and he is clearly not a writer in connection with whom it is appropriate to speak of apprentice work: his first book is an impressive achievement and he was 'by certain reviewers recognized as having arrived fully grown on the literary scene'. Though H. L. Mencken's later praise – 'I challenge . . . Christendom to point to another Opus 1 as magnificently planned and turned out' – may seem extravagant, *Almayer's Folly* is written with an assurance found in few first novels. Even more surprisingly, it is written in an English style that is for the most part free from lapses in idiom, and indeed, in many passages, remarkably expressive. Although the nineties are sometimes thought of as an age of aestheticism and literary decadence, a dominant mode in the fiction and drama of 1895 was a relentless social realism: it is the year of Hardy's *Jude the Obscure*, Grant Allen's *The Woman Who Did*, and Pinero's *The Second Mrs. Tanqueray*, as well as of Wilde's trial and imprisonment. There cannot be much doubt that the freshness of Conrad's exoticism and the absence of social propaganda were responsible for a large measure of his success.

As far as literary models are concerned, however, Conrad's first novel has affinities with more than one genre of fiction popular at the time. It is at once a love story, a novel of adventure, and an exercise in exoticism; and readers of the period would have been acquainted with this kind of fictional mixture in the work of such successful authors as R. L. Stevenson (who had left the way open for a successor by dying in 1894) and H. Rider Haggard. But, as Ian Watt persuasively argues, Conrad 'seems to follow, but actually undermines, the prescriptions of popular romance'. His hero is, as it turns out, an anti-hero; and though the plot incorporates many of the clichés of the romantic story of adventure, including a hidden treasure, a man-hunt, and a wrongly-identified corpse, the novel reads quite differently from, say, *Treasure Island* or *King Solomon's Mines*. This difference is, as Watt says, accounted for by 'the changeless torpor of Sambir and its symbolic representative, Almayer'.

In his sense of isolation and of being imprisoned by circumstances, Almayer anticipates many later Conradian protagonists. The narrator comments in Chapter 7 that 'The sense of his absolute loneliness came home to his heart with a force that made him shudder'; and two chapters later, when the Dutch lieutenant threatens to arrest him, Almayer himself exclaims: ' "Arrest! Why, I have been trying to get out of this infernal place for twenty years, and I can't" ', and adds a little later: ' "You think there is one dead man here? Mistake, I assure you. I am much more dead" '. Almost from the first, we realize that his dream of wealth and retirement to the Europe he has never seen is doomed to disappointment.

The setting for his despair and death is a small settlement in the tropical jungle; and throughout the novel the reader feels strongly the oppressive, almost claustrophobic quality of a 'nature' that is often hostile and menacing, usually indifferent to man's fate, and only occasionally in sympathy with his moods. (The novel in many passages neatly illustrates the thesis of Aldous Huxley's well-known essay 'Wordsworth in the Tropics'). A stylistic manifestation of this persistent theme is the frequent use of the pathetic fallacy, as in the following:

> A sigh as of immense sorrow passed over the land in the last effort of the dying breeze, and in the deep silence which succeeded, the earth and the heavens were suddenly hushed up in the mournful contemplation of human love and human blindness.

Ian Watt notes the 'Darwinian' element in the novel (a respect in which it anticipates *Heart of Darkness*) as well as the implications of 'biological determinism' in the treatment of Almayer's wife and

daughter. In the review already referred to, H. G. Wells identified
the 'central conception' of the novel as 'the relapse . . . from the
colonial version of civilization to a barbaric life' – another
anticipation of *Heart of Darkness.*

Frederick Karl has pointed out that Conrad's first novel
represents, structurally and technically, a break with
nineteenth-century traditions of English fiction:

> *Almayer's Folly,* similar in structure to the Flaubertian novel in
> which unity of plot predominates, is a radical departure from
> the multiple plots of the Victorians, and, along with *The Rover,* is
> perhaps the simplest of Conrad's novels. (*Reader's Guide,* p. 72)

AN OUTCAST OF THE ISLANDS

Conrad states that he was encouraged by Edward Garnett to embark on a second novel, and in his Author's Note to *An Outcast of the Islands* he recalls that, after meeting Garnett, 'on getting home I sat down and wrote about half a page of [the new novel] before I slept'. However, like some of Conrad's other recollections, this seems to have no basis in fact; for the novel seems to have been begun in August 1894, some four months after the completion of *Almayer's Folly* and some two months *before* his first meeting with Garnett. At that stage the novel was titled *The Two Vagabonds*. It was completed on 16 September 1895 and was published by Unwin in March 1896.

'You see that I can't get away from Malays. I am devoted to Borneo', Conrad had written to Marguerite Poradowska in August 1894; and the *Outcast* has a relation to *Almayer's Folly* that has been described by Frederick Karl as that of 'a sequel in reverse'. It has a similar setting and uses mainly the same characters, but the action is placed nearly twenty years earlier. The 'outcast', Peter Willems, has been described by Ian Watt as 'a somewhat more active, but very much more despicable, version of the youthful Almayer'. After being detected stealing from his employer and disgraced, he is given the chance to start again in Sambir, where he suffers an intense and desolating sense of isolation and rejection as well as being afflicted by

> ... the solid impassiveness of inanimate things; the big sombre-looking tree, the shut-up sightless house, the glistening bamboo fences, the damp and drooping bushes further off – all these things, that are condemned to look for ever at the incomprehensible afflictions or joys of mankind, assert in their aspect of cold unconcern the high dignity of lifeless matter that surrounds, incurious and unmoved, the restless mysteries of the ever-changing, of the never-ending life.

Willems finds a brief consolation in the arms of a beautiful native girl, Aissa, but afterwards betrays his benefactor, Lingard, to some Arab traders and is finally shot by Aissa. The story is thus a simple one but is spun out at considerable length: as Baines puts it, 'the chief difference between [Conrad's first two novels] is that *An Outcast of the Islands* is almost twice as long, and without any justification for being so'. Karl is another critic who notes a 'thinness and deficiency of substance': he sees the book as 'constructed with the force of an epic around an essentially puny centre. The conflicts of Willems, Lingard, Aissa and Almayer simply do not seem of sufficient import for their pretentious background'.

Contemporary reviewers for the most part greeted the novel enthusiastically; some spoke of 'singular power' and even of 'genius'. As with *Almayer's Folly*, the novelty of Conrad's setting and subject-matter made an impression: as a reviewer commented in the *Guardian* (10 June 1896), 'The story is fantastically unlike anything that would occur to European ideas'. A remarkable tribute was paid by H. G. Wells in the *Saturday Review* (16 May 1896): '*An Outcast of the Islands* is, perhaps, the finest piece of fiction that has been published this year, as *Almayer's Folly* was one of the finest that was published in 1895'. (Conrad responded by writing to Wells, and the review thus laid the foundation for their friendship.) Others, however, were critical of the slowness of the narrative and the prolixity of Conrad's style: the *National Observer* (18 April 1896; review probably by the editor, W. E. Henley) complained of his 'besetting sin of wordiness' and found his method 'diffuse' in comparison with the economy of Kipling. The latter had scored a success with his tales of the East from *Plain Tales from the Hills* (1888) onwards, and his name crops up frequently in early reviews of Conrad's work. The *National Observer* also invoked the name of Stevenson: 'It is like one of Mr Stevenson's South Sea Stories, grown miraculously long and miraculously tedious'.

Karl finds in the novel 'a dominant death theme': 'the jungle has gained in malevolence [compared with *Almayer's Folly*] and the sea is an ambivalent force of life and death'. It is chiefly notable for its presentation of Willems as a kind of Cain, a man apart from his fellows, physically and spiritually exiled and driven to self-destruction through the loss of his self-respect. Early in the novel he declares, ' "I shall never return. . . . I have done with my people. I am a man without brothers. Injustice destroys fidelity" '; and later his plight is revealed to the native woman:

> Her hands slipped slowly off Lingard's shoulders and her arms fell by her side, listless, discouraged, as if to her – to her, the savage, violent, and ignorant creature – had been revealed clearly in that moment the tremendous fact of our isolation, of the loneliness impenetrable and transparent, elusive and everlasting; of the indestructible loneliness that surrounds, envelopes, clothes every human soul from the cradle to the grave, and, perhaps, beyond.

This (from Part IV, ch. 3) sounds a note that is often to be heard again in Conrad's writing.

THE NIGGER OF THE 'NARCISSUS'

Conrad began work on this short novel in 1896. It was originally conceived as a story of 'about 30,000 words' (letter to Edward Garnett, 25 October 1896), but as so often with Conrad it expanded as he worked on it ('I am letting myself go with the *Nigger*. He grows and grows': 1 November 1896), and the length of the finished novel is just over 50 000 words. Not for the last time, composition was a painful business: he wrote to Garnett on 10 January 1897,

> Nigger died on the 7th at 6 p.m.; but the ship is not home yet. Expected to arrive tonight and be paid off tomorrow. And the end! I can't eat – I dream – nightmares – and scare my wife. I wish it was over!

It was finished within the next week, whereupon Conrad took to his bed for a couple of days – a small-scale version of the breakdowns he was later to suffer after the completion of some of his major works.

His emotional involvement in the book was considerable, and his desire for its artistic success correspondingly strong: he had told Garnett (25 October 1896) 'I must enshrine my old chums in a decent edifice'; the letter of 10 January 1897 quoted above continues, 'But I think it will do! It will do! – Mind I only think – not sure. But if I didn't think so I would jump overboard'; and after completion he confessed to Cunninghame Graham (9 August 1897), 'I am conceited about that thing and very much in love with it.' A little earlier he had written to Edward Sanderson (19 May):

> I am conceited enough about it – God knows, – but He also knows the spirit in which I approached the undertaking to present faithfully some of His benighted and suffering crea-

tures; the humble, the obscure, the sinful, the erring upon whom rests His Gaze of Ineffable Pity.

From August to December of the same year it was serialized in W. E. Henley's *New Review*; on 9 August Conrad asked Cunninghame Graham not to read it in the magazine version, since 'The instalment plan ruins it', but he naturally needed the double payment that came from serial and volume publication. On 30 November it was published in New York, under the (to American ears) less offensive title of *The Children of the Sea*, and on 2 December in London (the title-page of the English edition bearing the date 1898). Conrad had considered at least two other titles: *The Forecastle: a Tale of Ships and Men*, and *The Nigger: a Tale of Ships and Men*. In the serial version and the first American edition the subtitle was given as *A Tale of the Forecastle*, later amended to *A Tale of the Sea*.

Conrad was elated by the book's reception at the hands of reviewers: he noted that there were twenty-three reviews, most of them 'unexpectedly appreciative' (to Garnett, 7 January 1898), and Garnett referred to 'a general blast of eulogy from a dozen impressive sources'. Several reviewers, however, pointed out that the story possessed two curious features: the absence of plot and of female characters – 'no plot and no petticoats', as Israel Zangwill put in the *Academy* (1 January 1898; reprinted in *Critical Heritage*). Conrad had boldly chosen to dispense with these traditional and apparently indispensable ingredients of nineteenth-century fiction, a well-made plot and a strong romantic interest; and some of his critics were distinctly baffled. As Zangwill put it:

Up to a certain point it is refreshing to dispense with the love of women and the love of money, those hackneyed themes of the common novelist. But the writer who sets them aside assumes the responsibility of finding adequate substitutes, and this Mr Conrad has not succeeded in doing. His material is barely enough for half the number of pages, and he has not invented any *motif* that will lead the reader on from page to page.

This echoed complaints already made by other reviewers. The *Daily Mail*, for instance, had said (7 December 1897) that 'The tale is no tale, but merely an account of the uneventful voyage of the *Narcissus* from Bombay to the Thames', and the *Daily Telegraph*

(8 December 1897) that 'It is not a story at all, but an episode'. Arthur Symons (*Saturday Review*, 29 January 1898) was equally puzzled:

> . . . there is an almost endless description of the whole movement, noise, order, and distraction of a ship and a ship's company during a storm, which brings to one's memory a sense of every discomfort one has ever endured upon the sea. But what more is there? Where is the idea of which such things as these should be but servants?

A more appreciative reader was Conrad's fellow-novelist Arnold Bennett, who wrote to H. G. Wells (8 December 1897) that the book had

> moved me to enthusiasm. Where did the man pick up that style, & that *synthetic* way of gathering up a general impression & flinging it at you? Not only his style, but his attitude, affected me deeply. He is so consciously an artist.

As Conrad's phrase 'my old chums' (already quoted) indicates, and as at least one reviewer guessed, the story is based on personal experience, and indeed on a particular voyage. Even the ship's name is authentic: the *Narcissus* was a full-rigged sailing-ship on which Conrad had sailed as second mate from Bombay on 3 June 1884, arriving in Dunkirk on 16 October after an unusually long voyage of 136 days. Ian Watt states that

> In general . . . the action of *The Nigger of the 'Narcissus'* mainly follows the facts of the historical voyage, or deviates from them only in transferring or heightening events associated with other ships that Conrad had sailed on. There is a similar reliance on remembered experience as regards the characters. (p. 91)

One obvious change was the substitution of London for Dunkirk as the port of disembarkation; and there seems to have been no real-life parallel for the attempted mutiny. In most other respects Conrad kept close to his memories of people and events. A seaman actually did die during the voyage (on 24 September), though his name was not James Wait but Joseph Barron, and there is no firm evidence that he was a negro (Conrad told his biographer

Jean-Aubry that he had known a negro called James Wait on
another ship on which he served, but this seaman has not been
traced and Conrad's memory was very unreliable). Chapter 3 of
Watt's *Conrad in the Nineteenth Century* contains a detailed discussion of the factual background of the story.

The opening lines exhibit a masterly economy and directness,
and an unobtrusive blending of realism and poetic symbolism
that the late-twentieth-century reader, schooled by three generations of modernist and post-modernist writing, can take in his
stride, but that sorely perplexed or eluded many of Conrad's
earlier critics. (Among the other fiction of the same year was
Kipling's *Captains Courageous*, Wells' *The Invisible Man*, and
Maugham's *Liza of Lambeth*.) Conrad's manuscript shows how the
effect was strengthened from the earlier version:

> Mr Baker the chief mate of the ship 'Narcissus' came out of his
> cabin on to the dark quarterdeck. It was then just nine o'clock.

to the final text:

> Mr Baker, chief mate of the ship *Narcissus*, stepped in one stride
> out of his lighted cabin into the darkness of the quarter-deck.
> Above his head on the break of the poop, the night-watchman
> rang a double stroke. It was nine o'clock.

The weak 'came' has been replaced by the vigorous 'stepped in
one stride'; the auditory impact of 'rang a double stroke' has been
added to the flat statement of the time; most important of all, the
contrast of light and dark, already hinted in the title and soon to
become a dominant image, is stressed (it is to be reiterated in the
lines that follow, with their use of such phrases as 'a good lamp',
'streaks of brilliant light', 'the shadow of the quiet night',
'silhouettes of moving men', 'whiteclad Asiatics'). Conrad may
have had in mind a line from one of the most famous of English
poems, Coleridge's 'Ancient Mariner', which is also a tale of a
fateful sea-voyage: 'At one stride came the dark'.

In the pages that follow, the main characters of the story are
introduced – the narrator's use of the pronoun 'we' implies that he
is one of the crew and is recounting what he has seen at first hand –
and the antithesis of darkness and light, black and white, is
repeatedly prominent. Singleton has a 'white moustache', a

'white beard', and 'black-rimmed glasses'; he stands 'with his face to the light and his back to the darkness'. Belfast chews 'black tobacco', boasts of emptying a tar-pot over the white uniform of an officer, and curses ' "blast their black 'arts" '. Donkin wears a 'black coat', 'the white skin of his limbs showing his human kinship through the black fantasy of his rags'; he has 'white eyelashes' (the whiteness now unnatural and ominous), and takes refuge in the 'clean white forecastle'. Mr Baker, whose name perhaps suggests a floury whiteness (Conrad had actually known a first mate called Baker on the *Duke of Sutherland*), holds 'a white paper' for the roll-call. James Wait, the negro, appears spectrally in the chiaroscuro of the scene: 'The whites of his eyes and his teeth gleamed distinctly, but the face was indistinguishable'.

Wait's arrival is fraught with ambiguity and suggestiveness. His first word – his own surname – is misunderstood as an imperative and perhaps conveys a further wordplay, since he is to prove a weight or burden (and at the end, literally, a dead weight) before the voyage is over. His declaration ' "I belong to the ship" ' is as ominous as his ghastly cough, and no less ominous is the reference to the cook's later confession that ' "I thought I had seen the devil." ' Conrad's symbolism, however, is not simply a matter of polarities. Wait turns out to be the cause of disharmony, and almost of disaster, on the ship; but whatever first impressions are registered by the crew and reported by the narrator, he cannot ultimately or simply be identified with the forces of evil, since he is also a lonely, isolated figure. Wait is isolated both by his colour (Conrad said long afterwards that 'A negro in a British forecastle is a lonely being. He has no chums') and by the final solitude of the dying man. As such he demands our compassion.

The ship is named after a white flower, and at the beginning of the second chapter its appearance, 'all shining and white', is contrasted with that of the tug, like a 'black beetle', that tows her out of the harbour. (The immaculate ship and the shore-hugging beetle anticipate the symbolism of *Lord Jim*.) The ship is, up to a point, a microcosm of human life:

> She had her own future; she was alive with the lives of those beings who trod her decks; like that earth which had given her up to the sea, she had an intolerable load of regrets and hopes. On her lived timid truth and audacious lies; and, like the earth,

she was unconscious, fair to see – and condemned by men to an ignoble fate.

But only up to a point, for a page later Conrad writes that

The true peace of God begins at any spot a thousand miles from the nearest land; and when He sends there the messengers of His might it is not in terrible wrath against crime, presumption, and folly, but paternally, to chasten simple hearts – ignorant hearts, that know nothing of life, and beat undisturbed by envy or greed.

The 'peace of God' is, however, disturbed by the presence of Wait, who acts as a *memento mori*, reminding the crew by his words and his very presence that they too must some day die:

It was just what they had expected, and hated to hear, that idea of a stalking death, thrust at them many times a day like a boast and like a menace by this obnoxious nigger.

Conrad's irony plays on the paradox that Wait's claim to special treatment, to uniqueness, is based on that which unites and equalizes all men: the fact that we must all die.

Wait functions as a test of men's qualities: the crew are aligned and defined according to the attitudes they take up towards him, from Donkin's conviction that he is a fraud and his malicious delight in believing that his fellows have been duped, to Singleton's stoical observation that he had better get on with his dying quietly (as, in a sense, the elderly Singleton himself is doing). Wait undermines morale, the ambiguity of his state of health shaking the men's confidence (see the passage at the end of the second chapter: 'He fascinated us ... he trampled on our self-respect ...'). In his *Last Essays*, Conrad was later to state that the story depicted a crew 'brought to the test of what I may venture to call the moral problem of conduct'.

But Wait is not the only kind of test to which the crew are subjected, for the storm in chapter 3 is also a test of their qualities. When bad weather strikes, confidence is for a time restored: danger, and love of the ship, restore solidarity (that Conradian key-word, prominent in the Preface) and unite the men, who are now described as 'knitten together aft into a ready group by the first sharp order of an officer coming to take charge of the deck in bad weather'). In toil they both lose themselves and find themselves. As Albert Guerard says,

> The storm tests and brings out the solidarity, courage, and endurance of men banded together in a desperate cause. And the Negro James Wait tests and brings out their egoism, solitude, laziness, anarchy, fear.

The climax of this chapter is the rescue of Wait, who has been trapped in his cabin like 'a man prematurely shut up in a coffin'. Guerard sees this episode as 'central' to the story and, interpreting some of its details in terms of obstetric symbolism, suggests that 'the men have assisted at the rebirth of evil on the ship'. Certainly in the latter part of the story Wait is, in Guerard's words, *'something the ship and the men must be rid of before they can complete their voyage'* (again, Conrad's black sailor brings to mind Coleridge's white bird). Guerard also proposes a striking parallel with the story of Jonah, Conrad's 'A rage to fling things overboard possessed us' echoing Jonah 1:5 ('Then the mariners were afraid, and cried every man unto his god, and cast forth the wares that were in the ship into the sea').

The old sailor Singleton (his name perhaps suggesting single-mindedness as well as uniqueness) is a survivor of an earlier breed of seamen, as Conrad makes clear in his opening chapter: 'They [i.e. the older race of mariner] were the everlasting children of the mysterious sea. Their successors are the grown-up children of a discontented earth'. Later in the story he serves as an oracle, voicing the superstition that Wait is the cause of the unfavourable winds ('Mortally sick men – he maintained – linger till the first sight of land, and then die. . . . It is so in every ship': ch. 5). When it at last comes, the negro's death is brilliantly narrated: even the contemptible Donkin, sitting by the deathbed, is moved by the universal human realization that 'he himself, some day, would have to go through it all'. Wait's dying wish is that Donkin should ' "Light . . . the lamp" ' – but the lamp is already burning and the darkness that is overtaking him comes from within; as he dies, his eyes 'blaze up and go out at once, like two lamps overturned together by a sweeping blow'.

With the consigning of Wait's body to the deep, 'the ship rolled on as if relieved of an unfair burden' and completes its voyage. As the *Narcissus* enters its berth, 'a swarm of strange men, clambering up her sides, took possession of her in the name of the sordid earth. She had ceased to live'; and as the crew have come together in the opening pages of the story, so in its closing pages they disperse for ever. Wait's death has prefigured another kind of dying as the living organism of the ship's crew, united in a common task and shared dangers, disintegrates. The unsoundness of shore judgments is ironically exposed: the clerk in the shipping office deems Donkin 'an intelligent man' and Singleton ' "a disgusting old brute" ', but the reader knows better. Again the black/white, darkness/light antitheses assert themselves, giving a symmetry to the story: the men proceed from the *Narcissus* to the Black Horse, a riverside pub; the 'dark knot of seamen' stroll in the sunshine near the Mint, that symbol of shorebound values, 'white like a marble palace in a fairy tale' – or, we may think, a whited sepulchre.

The narrator, whose presence and identity have not been insisted on in the body of the tale, becomes prominent in these final paragraphs, and the concluding farewell, 'Good-bye, brothers! You were a good crowd . . .' – an oddly charitable envoi to a crew that has included Donkin and Belfast – is strongly personal. Technically, however, the narrative method is imperfect, since there have been scenes (notably those in Wait's cabin) conveying information that can hardly have been at the narrator's disposal. Frederick Karl judges Conrad 'lazy in his conception, or at least . . . not seriously concerned with the logic of his narration'. Conrad's more daring and more consistent experiments in first-person narration are still a little way ahead, though it may be noted that Marvin Mudrick's charge of 'gross violation of the point of view' in this story has been challenged by Ian Watt, who argues that 'The shifting point of view . . . enacts the varying aspects of its subject' (see *Nineteenth Century Fiction*, XII (1958); also the same critic's *Conrad in the Nineteenth Century*, p. 102).

The Nigger is, vividly, circumstantially and unforgettably, a tale of sailors, a ship, and the sea; but – what Conrad insisted on very early, but many of his early critics failed to recognize – it is also a good deal more than that. He told Helen Watson in a letter of 27 January 1897 that he had 'tried to get through the veil of details at the essence of life'. It follows from this (unless, of course, we choose to insist that he had no idea what he was up to) that the story should be allowed to unfold in the reader's mind, and that its details should not be subjected to any interpretation that limits their potential meaning. Ian Watt has rightly deplored the kind of *reductio ad symbolum* or grossly oversimplified symbolic interpretation that finds a one-to-one correspondence between character or incident and meaning, and that can only have the effect of narrowing and trivializing our understanding of Conrad's meaning and art: 'interpretation' that takes the form 'x stands for y', so far from penetrating beneath the surface of the text, has the effect of shutting off the reader's mind from a range of possible meanings. The story has several levels of meaning, none of which excludes or is excluded by the others. As Guerard has said:

> The story is indeed the tribute to the 'children of the sea' that Conrad wanted it to be: a memorial to a masculine society and the successful seizing of a 'passing phase of life from the remorseless rush of time' [quoted from Conrad's Preface]. It is certainly a tribute to this particular ship on which (for her beauty) Conrad chose to sail in 1884. But it is also a study in collective psychology; and also, frankly, a symbolic comment on man's nature and destiny: and also, less openly, a prose-poem carrying overtones of myth.

This is, as Guerard observes, 'no small burden', and it is hard to think of another prose tale written in England before the end of the nineteenth century (America, which had produced Hawthorne and Melville, is another matter) of which so much can with justice be claimed. Though the first of Conrad's sea stories, it remains one of his best. Jocelyn Baines' suggestion that it marks 'the culmination of Conrad's apprenticeship as a novelist' is surely too grudging: it is by any standards a major masterpiece and an extraordinary advance on his earlier books.

Less than four months before his death, Conrad wrote in a letter to Henry S. Canby (7 April 1924):

> . . . surely those stories of mine where the sea enters can be looked at from another angle. In the *Nigger* I give the psychology of a group of men and render certain aspects of nature. But the problem that faces them is not a problem of the sea, it is merely a problem that has arisen on board a ship where the conditions of complete isolation from all land entanglements make it stand out with a peculiar force and colouring.

This provides a complete rebuttal of the view of Conrad – common among his contemporaries (to his intense disgust) and still not extinct – as primarily a writer of sea stories. If much of his best work is 'about' ships and sailors, we still ought not to make the mistake of confusing his subject-matter with his underlying themes or of underestimating the scope of his enquiries into man's moral nature.

LORD JIM

Lord Jim was conceived as a short story to be included in the same volume as 'Youth', and the original subtitle was 'A Sketch' (later changed to 'A Tale'). In the course of composition it grew beyond all expectation, and it continued to grow even after the serial version was launched; but its origins can be traced in the unity of the finished novel. As Conrad told his publisher Blackwood on 18 July 1900, it presents 'the development of *one* situation, only *one* really from beginning to end'.

Exactly when work on *Lord Jim* began is not clear. Conrad's first reference to it is in a letter of 3 June 1898, at which time he envisaged it as a story of 'no less than 20–25 thousand words'. About a year later he referred to it as likely to amount to 'fully 40 000 words'. In October 1899, with composition still in progress, it began to appear as a serial in the prestigious monthly *Blackwood's Magazine*. At this time Conrad still believed that it would occupy only four or five instalments; in the event it was to run to fourteen, concluding only in November 1900. In late November 1899 Conrad thought the end was in sight; the following February he expressed a similar conviction – with twenty chapters completed at that time he apparently expected to finish off the story in another two chapters, though in fact it was to turn out to require another twenty-five. In May he admitted that it would run to '100 000 words or very little short of that'. The last pages were not written until 14 July, and the occasion is memorably described in a letter to John Galsworthy: Conrad worked continuously on the closing portion of the novel from nine in the morning on 13 July 1900 until dawn the next day, 'a steady drag of 21 hours'.

The novel is thus a remarkable instance of a book that grew far beyond the author's original intentions. The Patusan chapters were evidently an afterthought: as Ian Watt points out, if the book had ended at what is now chapter 22, Jim's time in Patusan would have had to be very perfunctorily treated: 'it seems certain that, a full five months after publication had begun, Conrad was still not thinking of giving the Patusan episode any extensive treatment, let alone the twenty-four chapters it eventually received'. In spite of personal and financial problems, Conrad appears to have been (as Thomas Moser has said) 'positively vibrating with creative energy' at this time. During the composition of *Lord Jim* he also wrote 'Youth' and 'Heart of Darkness' as well as some of *The Rescue*, in addition to his collaboration with Ford Madox Hueffer on *The Inheritors* and *Romance*.

The novel was published in volume form by Blackwood in October 1900 and appeared in America in the same year. (The Author's Note was not added until 1917.) It was favourably received by many reviewers, and Conrad went so far as to describe himself on 19 December 1900 as 'the spoiled child of the critics'. Several felt it to be his best work to date (his 'latest and greatest', according to the *Spectator*, on 24 November 1900), and the *Speaker* on the same day opined that it brought Conrad 'at once into the front rank of living novelists' – a remarkable tribute to one whose first book was only five years old. Henry James praised it in a letter (now lost) that Conrad described as 'absolutely enthusiastic'. Although more than one reviewer commended its originality, however, the novel's innovative method of narration was not to everyone's taste. The *Pall Mall Gazette* (5 December 1900) described the book as 'a very broken-backed narrative' – not the last time that the two-part structure was to be judged a weakness, though many modern critics have defended the structural coherence of the novel – and as 'tedious, over-elaborated, and more than a little difficult to read'. A reviewer in the *Sketch* (14 November 1900) declared it 'an impossible book – impossible in scheme, impossible in style', but was nevertheless constrained to admit that 'it is undeniably the work of a man of genius, of one who, wrongly I think, despises every popular and accepted method' (the reviewer was probably Oliver Onions, himself a novelist of a strictly traditional kind).

Conrad's story makes extensive use of actual events and personalities. (The sources have been thoroughly investigated by Norman Sherry, to whose *Conrad's Eastern World* the reader is referred for a detailed account.) On 17 July 1880, the steamship Jeddah left Singapore with nearly one thousand Muslim pilgrims on board, bound for Mecca. The ship was decrepit, ran into trouble, and on 8 August was abandoned by its European captain and officers, who believed it to be sinking and knew that the lifeboats were totally inadequate. Landing in Aden, they reported the ship lost with all its passengers; however, it turned up in Aden the very next day, having been found by another ship and towed into harbour.

The case was widely reported and attracted a great deal of attention: there was a court of inquiry at Aden, a question was asked in the House of Commons, and *The Times* and other London newspapers discussed it at length (the *Daily Chronicle*, for instance, referring to it as 'one of the most dastardly circumstances we have ever heard of in connection with the perils of the deep'). Conrad was in England at this time and must have first heard of the incident through the newspaper accounts. As a result of the official inquiry, Captain Clark had his certificate suspended for three years, and the chief officer, Williams, was severely reprimanded.

When Conrad arrived in Singapore on 22 March 1883, the *Jeddah*, still afloat, was among the ships in the harbour; and the sight of it, or waterside gossip, or both, must have revived memories of what he had read in London nearly three years earlier. But Conrad had a particular and personal reason for remembering the *Jeddah* case, which was, as Sherry has said, 'one of the most famous scandals in the East of the 1880s'. He had recently sailed from England on the *Palestine*, and when the cargo of coal caught fire (the episode recounted in 'Youth') the crew had taken to the boats. When he arrived in Singapore, Conrad was awaiting a court of enquiry, which in the event exonerated both master and crew. The affair of the *Palestine* was not of course precisely parallel to that of the *Jeddah*, but there was enough similarity to work on Conrad's conscience and his imagination.

At this time A. P. Williams, the former chief officer of the *Jeddah*, was living in Singapore (for details of his career, see 'A Conrad Who's Who' earlier in this volume). Sherry believes that Conrad met Williams and was sufficiently struck by the encounter to remember him and later base Jim upon him. Certainly the parallel between the two is striking: the prototype, like his fictional counterpart, was tall and powerfully built and dressed neatly in white; both worked as water-clerks after their disgrace, and married Eurasians; and Conrad's description of the parsonage that was Jim's home tallies quite closely with that of Porthleven, Cornwall, where Williams was born. At the same time there are important differences: Williams did not jump from the ship but was thrown overboard; and he remained in Singapore to the end of his days. As with Almayer and other characters based on real-life prototypes, Conrad did not hesitate to make changes – and it is easy to guess the reasons for the particular changes mentioned – in the process of transforming history into fiction, and it would be foolish to assume that the novel exactly mirrors his experience.

Like much of Conrad's fiction, *Lord Jim* contains elements of two quite different genres: the psychological novel and the story of adventure in an exotic setting. One of the obvious ways in which it differs from the traditional tale of adventure is in the complexity of the narrative method, which involves both a dislocation of straightforward chronology and the use of more than one narrative voice. The first chapter opens with a picture of Jim as a water-clerk, hints mysteriously at his recent history ('he would throw up the job suddenly and depart'), and after three paragraphs uncovering deeper layers of his experience goes back in time to his boyhood and to the ominous incident on the training-ship. The ensuing chapters narrate the *Patna* episode, culminating in the account of the court of inquiry in chapter 4, which concluded the first of the original instalments. The narrator of these opening chapters is unnamed and omniscient, but in chapter 5 his function is taken over by Marlow, who has been present at the court of inquiry, has struck up an acquaintance with Jim, and continues to follow his fortunes with interest in spite of the fact that they encounter each other only rarely. Marlow's narrative is presented as if partly spoken (chs 5–35) and partly written (chs 36–7). The spoken portion is said to have been delivered piecemeal, on various occasions and in various places:

> And later on, many times, in distant parts of the world, Marlow showed himself willing to remember Jim, to remember him at length, in detail and audibly. (ch. 4)

Marlow's narrative is punctuated from time to time by reminders of the speaker and his situation. Chapter 36 opens with the announcement that 'Marlow had ended his [spoken] narrative', and there follows a reference to a 'privileged man' who 'was [the] only one . . . of all these listeners who was ever to hear the last word of the story'. This man, who may conceivably be

identified with the narrator of the opening chapters, is the
recipient of a packet of papers 'more than two years later' than the
conclusion of Marlow's narrative; the packet includes a letter
from Marlow, another from Jim's father, a brief unfinished
message from Jim himself, and an account by Marlow ('as though
I had been an eye-witness') of the last phase of Jim's story. Even in
the earlier part of the novel, since Marlow's direct contact with
Jim is very limited, much of his narrative incorporates the briefer
narratives of others who were involved in specific episodes: thus
the 'elderly French lieutenant' who has served in the gun-boat
which discovers the *Patna* recounts his story to Marlow long
afterwards in the course of a chance meeting in Sydney (ch. 12),
and other parts of the story are told to Marlow by Jim himself (e.g.
chs 7–12). The cumulative effect is of a multiplicity of interlocking
or Chinese-box narratives: the 'frame' narrative of the opening
chapters accommodates Marlow's narrative, which in turn
accommodates the narratives of others. The shifting viewpoint
makes possible the vividness of first-hand accounts; at the same
time the presence of Marlow, dominant throughout most of the
novel, makes for cohesion. (Parallel to this is the reader's sense of
Conrad in complete control of a complex narrative structure that
appears to imitate the haphazard nature of experience – as in the
chance meeting in Australia of two men separately roaming the
globe and remaining together long enough to discover a common
interest and to swap yarns.)

Chronologically, the story makes few concessions to the traditional linear method of narration. By chapter 13, for instance, or
about a hundred pages into the novel, the reader is in a sense back
where he started on the opening page, with Jim employed as a
water-clerk. But only in a sense, for his knowledge of Jim and his
experiences has been greatly deepened. This zig-zag narrative
method is characteristic: in chapter 14 we are taken back to the
court of inquiry and its verdict; chapter 16 opens with a glimpse of
the future and of a Jim 'loved, trusted, admired'; chapter 18
expands the hint of the opening page by describing Jim's
wanderings and his succession of hastily-quitted jobs; and so
forth. There are large gaps in the story: Chapter 24 opens with a
jump of 'nearly two years', and shows Marlow visiting Patusan
and finding Jim settled there. It is, in all, a narrative method that
makes heavier demands on the patience and clearheadedness of
readers than most novelists writing in about 1900 required; but it

is of course not simply innovation for novelty's sake, but technique in the service of meaning. The mystery and glamour of Jim, and the interest he holds for the reader, are heightened by the narrative technique, which affords us not a consecutive narrative of his adventures that satisfies our curiosity but only occasional glimpses of his strange career separated by long intervals.

The book is also the story of a quest, or rather two quests. The more obvious one is Jim's search for adventure and self-fulfilment, a more inward version of the traditional tale of a search for hidden treasure or a lost civilization. The other is Marlow's psychological quest as he struggles towards an understanding of Jim, and this determines the principle of construction and narration. As Ian Watt points out, Conrad was developing further in *Lord Jim* a method he had used in an earlier Marlow story, 'Heart of Darkness':

> In both works the continuity of the narrative is based, not on the chronological sequence of actions as they occurred, but on the particular stage which Marlow has reached in his understanding of 'the fundamental why' of the moral puzzles presented by his tale. (p. 280)

Watt's chapter on his novel in *Conrad and the Nineteenth Century* contains a very full and clear discussion of the 'time shift' technique, which has also been labelled the 'chronological looping method' (see especially pp. 286–304).

J. E. Tanner has worked out an approximate chronology for the action of the novel ('The Chronology and the Enigmatic End of *Lord Jim*', *Nineteenth Century Fiction*, XXI (1966–7) pp. 369–80). He dates the 'Patna' incident in 1882 or 1883; Jim's arrival in Patusan three or four years later; Marlow's visit to Patusan two years after that; and Jim's death in 1889 or 1890. Since Jim was 'not yet four-and-twenty' at the time of the 'Patna' incident, he was born in about 1860 and was thus close to Conrad's own age. This supports Watt's suggestion that a 'major source of Jim is Conrad himself': author and character shared, for instance, 'youthful romantic dreams of heroic adventure'. Some have gone further and seen Jim's momentous jump from the *Patna* as a dramatization of Conrad's guilty preoccupation with his own quitting of his native land; this receives support from a phrase he later applied to his sudden departure from Poland – 'taking a standing jump out

of his racial surroundings and associations' – and it is also true
that the figure who 'jumps' out of a conventional and ordered way
of life is a recurrent one in his fiction.

As already noted, many critics have rejected the earlier charge
that *Lord Jim* is, structurally speaking, a novel that betrays the
curious circumstances of its composition by falling into two parts
that lack organic connection. They argue rather that the lengthy
Patusan episode, so far from being an uneasy addition, is an
integral part of the book.

As Douglas Hewitt says in *Conrad: A Reassessment:*

> In terms of plot there are undoubtedly two parts to the story:
> the defection of Jim and the disaster after he seems to have
> rehabilitated himself; certainly the second part has been added.
> But . . . they are intimately connected. It is, indeed, difficult to
> imagine the first part alone as a satisfactory story – certainly as
> a story by Conrad; the account of a cowardly leap for safety
> alone could hardly be enough; it demands development.

Hewitt suggests that signs of a 'change in conception' may be
discerned less in 'an untidy linking of an illogical second part'
than in 'a certain muddlement throughout, an uncertainty of the
final impression intended by Conrad'.

Jim's experiences, and his moral nature, dominate the entire
novel to a remarkable extent: there is no sub-plot, and every other
character is seen in relation to Jim – not only dramatically, in the
intermeshing of their experiences with his, but morally, in that
they nearly all make, explicitly or otherwise, a judgment of Jim's
nature. The French lieutenant, Gentleman Brown, Stein, even the
suicide Brierly, make their own comments, by word or deed, on
Jim's motives and actions, and in doing so 'place' themselves
morally in relation to him, from the almost god-like wisdom of
Stein to the 'satanic' temptations of Brown. When it comes to a
final judgment on Jim, however, we are on less sure ground, as
Douglas Hewitt's comment indicates. The same critic has
suggested that Marlow is 'bewildered' when he attempts to
understand Jim, and that Marlow's confusion mirrors that of
Conrad himself. A symptom of this is some of the rhetoric given to
Marlow, which is in places 'little more than a vague and rather
pretentious playing with abstractions'. Part of the problem
perhaps arises from the fact that Marlow's feelings towards Jim,

while to some extent quasi-paternal, also involve an element of self-identification: as Marlow says in Chapter 11, 'He was a youngster . . . of the sort you like to imagine yourself to have been'. Marlow feels (as Ian Watt says) 'nostalgia' for his own youth, and an ironic envy of, and pity for, Jim's idealism. At the same time, he cannot endorse Jim's actions, especially his irrevocable act of quitting the *Patna*, which is of the kind that threatens the 'solidarity of the craft' (Marlow uses this phrase in Chapter 11) and the moral code and professional ethic by which he lives.

Hewitt's conclusion is that Conrad's feelings in writing this book were 'too deeply and too personally involved for him to stand above the bewilderment in which he places Marlow'. This involvement is certainly borne out by the enigmatic closing words of the 'Author's Note' added in 1917: 'He was "one of us" '. The phrase 'one of us' echoes throughout the book, from Marlow's use of it very near the beginning of his narrative (chapter 5), to its appearance thirty-four chapters later. The phrase is protean and exemplifies in miniature the ambiguities of this novel – ambiguities that have been variously regarded as 'systematic' and an essential part of Conrad's complex meaning (this is the view expressed by Jacques Berthoud in his *Joseph Conrad*) or as proceeding from 'muddlement' (Hewitt's word).

There is a stimulating monograph on *Lord Jim* by Tony Tanner (1963), and the same critic's essay, 'Butterflies and Beetles – Conrad's Two Truths', in *Chicago Review*, 1963, can also be strongly recommended. The latter is reprinted, along with a judicious selection of other critical essays, in the Norton Critical Edition of *Lord Jim* edited by Thomas C. Moser (1968). Ian Watt's *Conrad and the Nineteenth Century* contains a long chapter on this novel.

NOSTROMO

Conrad's predictions, when he began work on *Nostromo*, that it would be 'something silly and saleable as "Youth" seems to be in a measure' (letter to Hueffer, 2 January 1903) and that it would be a 'story belonging to the "Karain" class of tales' (to Galsworthy, a little earlier) turned out to be very wide of the mark. The novel is his most ambitious undertaking, is often regarded as his masterpiece, and cost him enormous pains. As so often, he seems initially to have had no notion of the length and scope of the book that would take shape under his hands. As for the hope that it would be 'saleable', this – again as so often – was to be disappointed.

Progress during 1903 was hampered by illness and financial anxieties. On 23 March he described himself as 'a sick man'; on 26 May he wrote, 'I plod on drearily'; on 8 July he told Cunninghame Graham, a little more jauntily, 'I am dying over that cursed *Nostromo* thing.' By August he was able to tell his agent Pinker that he had written about 42 000 words; and in the same month he described the book to Galsworthy as 'half done' (and himself as 'half dead and wholly imbecile'). The letter to Pinker (22 August), however, shows signs of growing confidence:

> I have never worked so hard before – with so much anxiety. But the result is good. . . . You may take up a strong position when you offer it here. It is a very genuine Conrad. At the same time it is more of a Novel pure and simple, than anything I've done since *Almayer's Folly*.

He fell ill again later in the year, and at the end of 1903 wrote: 'If I had written each page with my blood I could not feel more exhausted at the end of this twelvemonth'. Najder (p. 291) offers an eloquent gloss to this quotation:

> At the time of writing *Nostromo* Conrad gave the impression of someone being wasted by a constant loss of blood, and from

among his statements about his ongoing work one could collect
a poignant anthology on authorial suffering.

As Baines points out, while there was undoubtedly a physical
basis (gout, probably aggravated by bad teeth) for Conrad's ill
health, there may well also have been a psychological factor.
There are interesting further references to the throes of composition in the Author's Note to the novel and in *A Personal Record*.

The later stages of composition saw no amelioration in
Conrad's state of mind. At the end of July 1904 he described
himself as 'half dead' and 'simply in despair'. Towards the end of
his task he was working 'practically night and day', and the final
portion was written in a long haul that took him all day and half
the night, the last words being written at 3 a.m. on 30 August.
Composition had thus occupied him for some twenty months.
After serialization during 1904 in *T.P.'s Weekly* (29 January–7
October), the book appeared, with a dedication to Galsworthy, on
14 October.

Years later, Conrad described the reception of *Nostromo* as 'the
blackest possible frost' (letter to Arnold Bennett, 25 November
1912). The *Times Literary Supplement* (21 October 1904) found the
novel 'disappointing' and 'not on a level with Mr Conrad's best
work': the reviewer declared that Conrad had 'succumbed to a
danger which must often have beset him – he has made a novel of a
short story' and suggested that 'the first two hundred pages of the
book' ought to have been 'ruthlessly cut'. John Buchan, reviewing
it in the *Spectator* (19 November 1904), found in it 'the characteristic merits and defects' of Conrad's work but judged the story 'of
surpassing interest', even though he was obviously disconcerted
by the narrative method ('the construction of the book is
topsy-turvy, beginning in the middle and finishing at the start').

Conrad's gloom over the book's critical reception was not
altogether justified; actually it received, as Norman Sherry points
out, 'a good deal of commendation', and it seems (to quote Sherry
again) that Conrad 'forgot the praise but remembered the
criticism'. The *Illustrated London News* review began handsomely:
'To say that *Nostromo* is the great achievement in fiction of the year
is to state altogether imperfectly our appreciation of Mr Conrad's
latest novel' (26 November 1904); and Edward Garnett published
a long and perceptive review in the *Speaker* (12 November 1904;
reprinted in *Conrad: The Critical Heritage*). Apart from the length of

the novel, Conrad's narrative method seems to have been the main stumbling-block for many reviewers: thus a reviewer in the *British Weekly* (10 November 1904), while finding the novel 'excellent' as a whole, deemed the story 'not well told', and remarked somewhat bemusedly: 'The plot is confused; the tale does not run smoothly from incident to incident; it is often difficult to say when or where we are'. All the more credit, then, to Arnold Bennett, who was often a shrewd and sympathetic reader of Conrad and delighted him in 1912 by declaring: 'When I first read it I thought it the finest novel of this generation (bar none), and I am still thinking so.'

Among more recent critics, F. R. Leavis's view, expressed in *The Great Tradition* (1948), that *Nostromo* is Conrad's 'most considerable work' and 'one of the great novels of the language' has been influential. For Albert J. Guerard, too, it is Conrad's 'greatest achievement', while Baines finds it 'worthy of comparison with . . . *War and Peace*'. This is not to say that it is the most widely-read of Conrad's books (school examination syllabuses, perhaps understandably, fight shy of it), for it presents undeniable difficulties to the reader. These are, in the main, difficulties of method rather than of subject-matter or ideas; but before examining them more closely the world of *Nostromo* may be briefly described.

Leavis, having characterized Conrad as 'the laureate of the Merchant Service, the British seaman happily doubled with the artist', notes that *Nostromo* 'complicates the account of Conrad's genius' and requires a drastic modification of that 'formula'. Here – as again a little later in that other major masterpiece *The Secret Agent* – Conrad abandoned the sea, ships and sailors as his subject-matter and in doing so renounced the autobiographical sources on which he had drawn so heavily and so fruitfully in most of his earlier writings, and was to draw again, less fruitfully, in his late novels. The setting of *Nostromo* is a South American republic; but of that region Conrad had only the flimsiest experience, dating from 1876, when he briefly visited the ports of Cartagena in Colombia and Puerto Cabello and La Guaira in Venezuela while serving as a steward on the barque *Saint Antoine*. As Najder says, 'Several days on land provided Conrad with the visual material for *Nostromo*'. The main sources of the novel are literary rather than personal, and the creation of Costaguana is a feat of imagination rather than recollection. Although attempts have been made to identify it with one or other of the South American republics, it seems to be no mere transcription from reality: to quote Norman Sherry, 'Costaguana, and particularly Sulaco, are seen to be made up of hints from areas all over South America', and even the place-names are borrowed from various sources (for example, Sulaco is in Honduras; Santa Marta in Colombia; Zapiga in Chile; Esmeralda in Ecuador). Sherry's *Conrad's Eastern World* (1971) furnishes a full and fascinating account of the sources of the novel, including the use of real-life prototypes for such characters as Nostromo and Decoud.

According to Conrad's 'Author's Note', the germ of the novel was a 'vagrant anecdote' about a sailor 'who was supposed to have stolen single-handed a whole lighterful of silver'. From this germ grew the action of the novel, the character of Nostromo, and the dominant symbol of the silver-mine. Conrad consulted a number of historical and topographical works on various South American countries, and (as Sherry demonstrates in detail) drew material from them that appears in his novel. But these debts in no way lessen his achievement in creating a highly specific and consistent account of a city and a country (Leavis comments that 'Sulaco . . . is brought before us in irresistible reality').

If 'silver' is one of the key-words of the novel, 'material interests' is one of its key-phrases; and Juliet McLauchlan has noted in her useful monograph on *Nostromo* (1969) that many of the characters are 'defined . . . in terms of their attitude to material interests': among them are Gould, Nostromo, Holroyd, Sir John, and Captain Mitchell. Another group that includes Mrs Gould, Monygham, Giorgio, Decoud and Don Jose are, in contrast, 'free from direct material interest'. But within these two broad categories, Conrad makes careful and important discriminations. Of Captain Mitchell, for instance, McLauchlan writes:

As the faithful servant of his company, his connection with material interests is close, but he cannot paradoxically be said to be corrupted by them, since he has integrity which no corruption can touch. Yet his lack of imagination and blindness to the significance of events around him mean that he unquestioningly accepts the progress of material interests in Costaguana and is naively delighted with the power of the mine. He is corrupt because his judgment is corrupt. His ideal of duty, genuine in itself, is flawed, or becomes an illusion, in that he is serving something much less worthy than he believes.

Leavis states that the 'main political, or public, theme' of *Nostromo* is 'the relation between moral idealism and "material interests" '.

The reader's difficulty in coming to terms with this novel on a first reading largely result from Conrad's use of the 'time-shift' already referred to in the discussion of *Lord Jim* above. It is possible to extract from the text a fairly simple and clear chronology of events covering a considerable period of time. There are references to the coming of the Spanish conquistadores; to the three generations of the Gould family who have lived in Costaguana; and to the public events, both historical and fictitious, that form a background to the private experiences recounted (for example, Charles Gould's grandfather has fought with the great patriot Bolivar in the early nineteenth century). More recent events are often dated with some precision, and Conrad evidently took pains to achieve internal consistency. He does not, however, narrate events in the order of their occurrence, but cuts frequently, and sometimes disconcertingly, from one scene to another with strides or leaps backwards or forwards in time, the precise extent of the time-shift not always being immediately evident. These shifts can occur from chapter to chapter, or within a single chapter (e.g. the flashback in the second chapter of the novel, introduced by the words, '. . . on a memorable occasion he Captain Mitchell had been called upon to save the life of a dictator'; this flashback continues throughout chapter 3, and only in Chapter 4 do we return – and even then not consistently – to the time-period in which chapter 2 opened).

These time-shifts serve several purposes. At the simplest level they enable the novelist to appear to avoid (it is, arguably, no more than an appearance or illusion) the kind of artificiality associated with the chronological recital of the Thackerayan or Trollopian variety in which an omniscient narrator unfolds a tale of events long past and done with. For the deliberateness and detachment of the traditional story-teller, Conrad substitutes what *seems* to be a capricious, unpredictable method of narration resembling that of genuine oral narrative, where one disclosure suggests another that is associated with it by something other than chronological proximity. Such a method also stimulates the reader's curiosity as to cause and effect: from knowing how things turn out at a later stage, we naturally wish to learn how they started. Furthermore, the method makes possible juxtapositions that create a powerful effect of irony: one example of this (noted by Leavis) is when Conrad shows the failure of the Ribierist regime *before* he describes its ideals at the outset, so that the shadow of its outcome is cast over its earlier phases.

C. B. Cox's volume in the 'Casebook Series', *'Heart of Darkness'*, *'Nostromo'* and *'Under Western Eyes'* (1981), brings together some of the most important critical discussions of this novel.

THE SECRET AGENT

In the long and interesting 'Author's Note' that Conrad wrote for an edition of *The Secret Agent* in 1920, thirteen years after the novel's original publication, he states that it was begun 'impulsively' and written 'continuously'. His first reference to it is on 21 February 1906, when he sent his literary agent, J. B. Pinker, thirteen pages of what was intended to be a short story titled 'Verloc'. *Nostromo* had been recently finished, and Conrad had again taken up *Chance*; but he laid it aside to work on a new venture, which evidently seized his imagination strongly, and a version of *The Secret Agent* was finished by early November, serialization in an American magazine (*Ridgway's: A Militant Weekly for God and Country*) having already begun on 6 October (it ran until 12 January 1907). As these facts show, the notion of a short story was quickly abandoned as Conrad found his original conception growing beneath his hand. By 5 March, indeed, less than two weeks after his first mention of 'Verloc', he refers to it as 'a longish story: 180 000 words or so' – in anticipation, that is, for in the final version it was to turn out to be about 105 000 words, or not much more than half of that figure.

Conrad seems not to have had a high opinion of the serial version: he told Galsworthy (12 September) that he 'must not take it too seriously. The whole thing is superficial and it is but a tale', and insisted to another correspondent (7 November) that it had 'no social or philosophical intention'. He recognized that much more work would be required before it could appear in volume form, and soon set to work to revise and expand the serial version, so that he was able to tell Galsworthy on 30 July 1907 that between mid-May and mid-July he had written another 28–30 000 words 'in order to make a decent book of *The Secret Agent*'. This final version was published in London and New York in September. The revision had coincided with a very difficult, even traumatic, period in Conrad's domestic life: apart from the usual money troubles, he had been racked with anxiety and exhausted with nursing his two sons, who had been seriously ill during a period of residence abroad. As he told Galsworthy, 'It has been altogether a ghastly time'.

The critical reception of the novel was generally favourable, and it was praised in such prestigious weeklies as *The Spectator*, *The Times Literary Supplement*, and *The Nation*. This last review was by Edward Garnett, who delighted Conrad by spotting the significance of Winnie's mother: 'the real heroine of the story is concealed in the trivial figure of Mr Verloc's mother-in-law'. Conrad wrote to him on 1 October: 'I am no end proud to see you've spotted my poor old woman. You've got a fiendishly penetrating eye for one's most secret intentions. She *is* the heroine'. Garnett's perceptiveness may be contrasted with the obtuseness of a hostile reviewer in *Country Life*, who described the account of her departure as 'an excrescence'. The book also received some favourable reviews in America. But the *New York Times Book Review*, while praising Conrad's art, noted that 'he is able to write of woman without investing her with a shred of romance. Therefore, he is cut off from the wider popular favor', and in the event the novel did not sell. Early in the new year, Conrad told Galsworthy that it 'may be pronounced by now an honourable failure', and confessed that he was 'cast down'.

The Secret Agent shared in the general neglect of Conrad's work during the generation after his death, though Edward Crankshaw suggested in his 1936 book that in it he 'achieved what may have been the greatest of all his purely technical feats'. Its recognition as a masterpiece, and one of the finest of all Conrad's novels, came with the appearance of F. R. Leavis's *The Great Tradition* in 1948, in which Conrad is awarded one of the five places in the pantheon of English fiction and this particular book is declared to be 'one of the two unquestionable classics of the first order that he added to the English novel' (the other is *Nostromo*).

Conrad's manuscript is now in Philadelphia (Phillip H. and A. S. W. Rosenbach Foundation Museum and Library). Towards the end of his life, he made two dramatic versions of *The Secret Agent*: one in four acts was privately printed in 1921, the other in three acts was produced at the Ambassadors' Theatre, London, on 2 November 1922, but ran for only a few nights. (Conrad wrote wryly of the 'touching unanimity' of the critics in 'damning the play'.) For details of Alfred Hitchcock's 1936 film version, see under 'Filmography' later in this volume.

As Norman Sherry has said, 'Conrad's imagination required always a firm basis of fact'. *The Secret Agent* undoubtedly has such a basis, but the situation is confused by the mutually inconsistent statements made at various times by Conrad himself. In a letter of 7 November 1906, he stated that the story was 'based on the inside knowledge of a certain event in the history of active anarchism'. In the 'Author's Note' of 1920, he offers quite a full account of the origins of the novel. 'The subject of *The Secret Agent*,' he says there, '. . . came to me in the shape of a few words uttered by a friend in a casual conversation about anarchists or rather anarchist activities'; the friend was Ford Madox Hueffer, and Conrad adds that, in the course of a discussion on this subject, 'we recalled the already old story of the attempt to blow up the Greenwich Observatory', and that Ford had remarked, 'Oh, that fellow was half an idiot. His sister committed suicide afterwards.' The incident referred to is the so-called 'Greenwich Park Explosion' of 14 February 1894. Whether the conversation took place as reported is open to question: Conrad was a highly unreliable recorder of the past at the best of times, and here he was claiming to reproduce words spoken some fourteen or fifteen years earlier. In 1923 he denied all knowledge of the 'Greenwich Bomb Outrage', claimed that he was out of England at the time (he was not), and insisted that his novel was 'in intention, the history of Winnie Verloc' (though the original title was *Verloc*). Sherry, whose admirably detailed account of the background to the novel will be found in his *Conrad's Western World*, suggests that he was trying to cover his creative tracks by concealing his sources of information. Certainly it seems likely that he knew at the time of the explosion, which was widely reported in the newspapers.

One partial explanation of these inconsistencies is that Conrad was reacting to a shift that genuinely took place in the main thrust of the novel. Although it may have begun as a tale of anarchists with Verloc as a grubby protagonist (Winnie is less prominent in the serial version than she later became), in its final form it is arguably a study of relationships in which Winnie is dominant and the anarchist theme sinks into the background. This kind of shift might have seemed to Conrad to justify his repudiation of his earlier debts and would be consistent with Ian Watt's observation that 'although Joseph Conrad's fiction nearly always started from some germ of reality – an anecdote, an historical event, an incident seen or a conversation overheard – by the time the work was finished it usually disclaimed any relation to actual persons, places or events.' While there is in this case a discernible substructure of mysterious and grisly historical events, the most important aspects of the book justify its being regarded as (in Conrad's own phrase) 'a work of imagination'.

In its evocation of the squalor and brutality of lower-class life in the metropolis, *The Secret Agent* owes something to Dickens, and in its combination of this element with a story of espionage and political intrigue it represents the side of Conrad that was to be an important influence on Graham Greene. The title has a consciously lurid quality and seems to offer a different book from the one we are in fact given; the subtitle, 'A Simple Tale', seems to reinforce, or perhaps to undermine, the title's promise; but we cannot read very far into the book without realizing that both are ironically intended. As a representative of the romantic profession of spy, Mr Verloc is a joke; and, despite its melodramatic surface, the tale turns out to be anything but simple. From the title onwards, indeed, the novel is permeated by a remarkably consistent irony that gives depth and complexity. As F. R. Leavis has said:

> The matter, the 'story', is that of a thriller – terrorist conclaves, embassy machinations, bomb-outrage, detection, murder, suicide; and to make, in treating such matter with all the refinements of his craft, a sophisticated moral interest the controlling principle is, we recognize, characteristic Conrad.

One stylistic pointer to the persistent 'moral interest' (sometimes in combination with the pervasive irony) is the recurrence of the word 'morality' and its cognates in such phrases as 'moral efficiency', 'abstract morality', 'moral nature', 'moral corruption', 'moral agent of destruction'.

The subtlety of Conrad's method becomes clear from a careful reading of the very first page of the novel. At first glance, the manner seems guilelessly straightforward ('The shop was small, and so was the house') in a manner we might associate with the scrupulous realism of Arnold Bennett (*The Old Wives' Tale* appeared in the following year). But Conrad's art of the suggestive and the oblique is already very much in evidence: phrases such as 'very little business', 'ostensible business', 'in charge of his brother-in-law', 'discreetly but suspiciously ajar', 'either for economy's sake or for the sake of the customers' either mean more than they appear to be saying or (as in the case of the last phrase quoted) suggest a sly or teasing ambiguity. Irony, ambiguity, paradox: these are to be the dominant modes of the novel, manifested on many levels, from the comic incongruity of Verloc's profession and his marriage (he is a 'thoroughly domesticated' anarchist) to the terrible trick of fate by which Winnie's mother, having condemned herself to misery for her son's sake, is indirectly the cause of his death.

As already noted, in some of its aspects – notably its settings – *The Secret Agent* shows the influence of Dickens. In *A Personal Record* Conrad not only refers to a translation of *Nicholas Nickleby* as having been almost his 'first introduction to English imaginative literature' but singles out *Bleak House* for praise as

> a work of the master for which I have such an admiration or rather such an intense and unreasoning affection, dating from the days of my childhood, that its very weaknesses are more precious to me than the strength of other men's works. I have read it innumerable times both in Polish and in English.

In his 'Author's Note', Conrad describes the way in which the world of *The Secret Agent* imaginatively presented itself to him:

> Then the vision of an enormous town presented itself, of a monstrous town more populous than some continents and in its man-made might as if indifferent to heaven's frowns and smiles; a cruel devourer of the world's light. There was room enough there to place any story, depth enough for any passion, variety enough there for any setting, darkness enough to bury five millions of lives.

This is very close to the world of *Bleak House*, where Dickens depicts the metropolis as a vast jungle in which countless separate, but unknowingly interconnected, lives are lived; and while Conrad does not aim at a Dickensian sociological comprehensiveness, his rendering of the physical and moral aspects of the city is comparable, just as his reference in the 'Author's Note' to 'my solitary and nocturnal walks all over London in my early days' recalls Dickens' own habit of night-walking through London's deserted streets.

As Frederick Karl has pointed out in his interesting short essay 'Conrad's Debt to Dickens' (*Notes & Queries*, ccii, 1957), 'Conrad's description of London is never very far from the grimy London of Dickens' novels'. The novel depicts an urban landscape of dirt and gloom, in which physical objects seem on the point of disintegration and even animate creatures sometimes share this quality. In its opening pages, Mr Verloc's house is 'grimy', the shop-bell is 'hopelessly cracked', and his customers' clothes are 'much worn', and the neighbourhood abounds in 'narrow alleys' and 'unsavoury courts': we are not far from the foul slum of Tom-All-Alone's in *Bleak House*, though Winnie has been successful (but only just so) in preventing herself and those she loves from being engulfed by the tide of squalor and misery. The street is 'sordid', all around stretches 'the enormity of . . . bricks', and the moral confusion is symbolized, as in the opening pages of *Bleak House*, by a 'raw, unwholesome fog'.

It may be added that there are also some recognizably Dickensian touches in characterization, episode, and style. Characters such as Mr Vladimir come close to caricature; some of the namings are symbolic (Chief Inspector Heat recalling Dickens' detective, Mr Bucket); and there is a similar use of real-life prototypes (Sir William Harcourt is the original of the Home Secretary, Sir Ethelred, who is introduced with a strongly Dickensian passage of description). One of the finest scenes in the book, the cab-ride that consigns Winnie's mother to a lonely death, is reminiscent of Dickens. (It also recalls a short story by Chekhov, 'Heartache', but I do not know any evidence that Conrad was familiar with the story.) It has been pointed out that G. K. Chesterton's novel *The Man who was Thursday* (1908) reads very much like a counterblast to *The Secret Agent*.

Ian Watt's volume on *The Secret Agent* in the 'Casebook Series' (1973) brings together some of the most notable critical discussions and also contains a long and valuable critical survey.

UNDER WESTERN EYES

Towards the end of 1907 Conrad began work on a novel at that time titled *Razumov*. Work continued through 1908 and 1909, and the book was finished by the end of the latter year. Its completion was marked by a serious physical and emotional breakdown that laid Conrad low for several months in the early part of 1910: during his delirium, his wife wrote, the manuscript lay near his bed and 'he lives mixed up in the scenes and holds converse with the characters' (letter of 6 February 1910). As he recovered he was able to embark on revisions, which involved substantial excisions from the 1357-page manuscript (Conrad speaks of 'cutting down that novel ruthlessly'). It was serialized in the *English Review*, and simultaneously in the *North American Review*, from December 1910 to October 1911, appearing in volume form in the latter month. Between serial and volume there were further excisions, the final version being some 30 000 words shorter than the serial. The book was dedicated to Agnes Tobin. A projected dramatic version a few years later came to nothing.

The novel won high praise from some of its reviewers. The *Pall Mall Gazette* (11 October 1911) praised its 'amazing truth' and 'varied and masterly characterisation'. Richard Curle, who was later to become a close friend and one of Conrad's more important early critics, declared in the *Manchester Guardian* (11 October 1911) that 'A new work by Mr Conrad is a literary event of the first importance' and found *Under Western Eyes*, 'though not one of Mr Conrad's typical achievements', 'a remarkable book'. The *Morning Post* (12 October 1911) judged it 'a perfectly poised work of art' and the author's finest achievement since *Lord Jim*. Gratifying as all this must have been, it did not bring what Conrad really yearned for and needed at this time – popular recognition, commercial success, and freedom from nagging financial anxieties.

Not surprisingly, some of the earliest critics stressed the political and international aspects of the book. For a reviewer in the *Westminster Gazette* (14 October 1911), for instance, it was 'a brilliantly successful effort to make the Russian comprehensible to the Westerner'. Edward Garnett suggested in the *Nation* (21 October 1911) that Conrad owed a debt to Turgenev and Dostoievsky. The novel seems to have put a strain on Garnett's friendship with Conrad: as a Slavophile, Garnett reacted against the bitterly hostile picture of Russian autocracy and wrote a private letter of protest to Conrad; although the letter has not survived, we can guess its drift from Conrad's reply (20 October 1911), which refers to his being 'charged with the rather low trick of putting one's hate into a novel' and retorts: 'Is it possible that you haven't seen that in this book I am concerned with nothing but ideas . . . ?'.

Under Western Eyes presents the favourite Conradian theme of isolation: its protagonist begins as a student without family (as Tony Tanner says, 'Being a disowned bastard he is perpetually in that unfettered, unmoored, alienated state which Conrad found the crucial testing time for a man'), and ends as a deaf man shut off within himself from the world. It also, like *Lord Jim*, presents the theme of guilt and atonement: as Baines points out, 'There is a similarity between Razumov's action and Jim's jump from the pilgrim ship. They were both acts of cowardice committed in exceptional circumstances by unexceptional people with average moral sensibility'. But as well as examining the response of an individual to the demands made upon him by fate, the novel offers a picture, and a criticism, of a nation and a society; and again, as the title suggests, the method resembles that of *Lord Jim* in that 'the events are registered through the "western eyes" of the elderly teacher of languages, and it is his comments, like those of Marlow [in the earlier book], that draw out the moral significance' (Baines). It is not merely, as Conrad describes it at one point, 'a Russian story for Western ears' but a Russian story filtered through a Western consciousness that frequently protests its own inability to understand the Russian nature ('no comprehension of Russian character'). Douglas Hewitt makes the interesting distinction that 'the teacher of languages resembles the Marlow of *Chance* rather than the Marlow of *Heart of Darkness*. He is not personally involved in the fate of Razumov; nothing new in his own character is brought to the surface by his knowledge of the Russian's treachery and remorse'.

The reference above to 'guilt and atonement' as a theme of the novel inevitably recalls Dostoeivsky's *Crime and Punishment*. Conrad had little regard for Dostoievsky – he found *The Brothers Karamozov* 'terrifically bad and impressive and exasperating . . . like some fierce mouthings from prehistoric ages' – and must have been little pleased by Garnett's suggestion of influence. In any case, apart from the superficial similarities of setting and situation, the two books have little in common: as Baines reminds us, the Russian novelist's faith in the goodness of God and his emphasis on repentance and redemption have no parallel in Conrad, whose attitude is unambiguously fatalistic and ironical.

Present-day estimates of the novel are generally high, though not without reservations. For Leavis, though inferior to *The Secret Agent*, it is 'a most distinguished work' which 'must be counted among those upon which Conrad's status as one of the great English masters securely rests'. Thomas Moser places it as the 'last of the political novels and of the major, full-length novels'. Baines finds the characters 'more subtly and convincingly developed than those in any other of Conrad's novels': 'Razumov himself is the most considerable character that Conrad created' and Natalia Haldin is 'Conrad's most effective portrait of a woman'. This last verdict has not commanded universal assent, and the women characters in general have been found weak by some critics. Moser points out that there was a significant shift in Conrad's intentions regarding the relationship between Razumov and Natalia: whereas Razumov's love for the sister of the man he had betrayed was originally to have been 'the center of the novel', in the final version it occupies only some ten per cent of the total.

Other criticisms have been that the great achievement of the opening chapters is not sustained throughout the book, and that Conrad's completely understandable hostility to Russia leads him to lack objectivity. A technical weakness has also been diagnosed in Conrad's narrative method, C. B. Cox, for instance, finding the use of the teacher of languages to be 'a most unsatisfactory device'. Some of the problems are those inherent in the use of an eye-witness, such as affording him plausible access to the information he must relay: thus Cox complains that 'His presence during the confession scene between Razumov and Natalia is embarrassing', and not unreasonably echoes the former's comment, ' "How did this old man come here?" ' But due allowance must be made for a convention that, however artificial (and how, in a work of art, can it be otherwise?), is most of the time accepted as readily as other conventions of fiction and drama. Cox's complaint that there is inconsistency in the complacent and dull narrator's possessing a 'grasp of language and astute powers of artistic selection' has a ready answer: a novelist who wishes to be read will hardly take pains to make his narrative style uniformly complacent and dull, and somewhat similar objections can be raised against other narrators such as Esther Summerson in *Bleak House* and Nelly Dean in *Wuthering Heights*. Conrad achieves considerable ironic force by putting this tale of tyranny and betrayal into the mouth of (in Cox's words) a 'modest, decent, tolerant liberal' unable to comprehend the depths of his own narrative. As in many first-person narratives (*Huckleberry Finn* comes to mind), the reader sees much more than the narrator is aware of conveying. In a very interesting discussion of the nature and role of the narrator, Tony Tanner has suggested that 'One major effect of the book is to secure a qualifying judgment on the myopia of those western eyes': for Tanner, in other words, the teacher's fatuous imperceptiveness constitutes a criticism of 'western common-sense and complacency'.

Tanner's long essay appeared in the *Critical Quarterly*, III, 1962, and is reprinted, along with the discussions by Hewitt and Moser also referred to above, in the Casebook on *Heart of Darkness*, *Nostromo* and *Under Western Eyes* edited by C. B. Cox (1981). Cox's own consideration of this novel is contained in his *Joseph Conrad: The Modern Imagination* (1974). There is also relevant material in Eloise Knapp Hay's *The Political Novels of Joseph Conrad* (Chicago, 1963) and Norman Sherry's *Conrad's Western World* (1971).

CHANCE

By the time Conrad finished *Chance* in March 1912 he had been at work on it intermittently for some seven years. He seems to have begun it in 1905, soon after completing *Nostromo*, but progress had for a long time been slow and often interrupted by other commitments. A boost to its composition and completion came when, in the summer of 1910, he was invited to contribute a serial to the *New York Herald*, a leading newspaper. This was an opportunity not to be missed, and indeed its serialization was probably a factor in Conrad's marked change of fortunes brought about by *Chance*. It appeared in the *Herald* from 21 January to 30 June 1912; extensive revisions were then made before its publication in volume form at the beginning of 1914. There was no serial appearance in England.

Conrad had a high opinion of the novel – he told his agent Pinker, 'It's the biggest piece of work I've done since *Lord Jim*' – but bitter experience had taught him to be (as he says in the same letter of 2 June 1913) 'much less confident' about the public reaction. He certainly longed for success at this point in his career: after nearly twenty years as a professional author, and despite golden opinions from many of the critics, the income from his writings was still very modest. On the other hand, it would be unfair to Conrad to suggest that he was willing to purchase success at any price; and although there may be some concessions to popular taste in *Chance* (in, for example, the happy ending), one does not have a sense that he was deliberately writing down to a mass audience, and in some respects it is a novel that places difficulties in the way of the reader (for example, in its narrative method). Moreover, there is evidence that Conrad had a genuine wish to win readers for other than commercial reasons: in the 'Author's Note' he writes that

What I always feared most was drifting unconsciously into the position of a writer for a limited coterie; a position which would have been odious to me as throwing a doubt on the soundness of my belief in the solidarity of all mankind in simple ideas and in sincere emotions.

The same sentiment is echoed in a letter a few years later (21 December 1918):

I am sufficient of a democrat to detest the idea of being a writer of any 'coterie' of some small self-appointed aristocracy in the vast domain of art or letters . . . want to be read by many eyes and by all kinds of them, at that.

In the event, *Chance* was, by Conrad's standards, a notable success with the public, selling 13 200 copies in the first two years – more than three times the sales of his previous novel, *Under Western Eyes*. It may be, as some writers on Conrad have suggested, that its success was the inevitable result of a gradual process: his fame had been mounting, and his claims to be regarded as one of the leading novelists of the day had been repeated, for some time; and wider recognition was due if not overdue. But there are also specific features of *Chance* that qualified it for popular success. Conrad himself shrewdly noted that 'It's the sort of stuff that *may* have a chance with the public. All of it about a girl and with a steady run of references to women in general all along'. Apart from the happy ending and the strong feminine element (it even had a girl on the dust-jacket – a stroke that Edward Garnett believed responsible for some of the sales), it reintroduced Marlow and thus brought Conrad's earlier work back into the minds of his older readers. Many readers seem to regard with disapproval, or at least disappointment, any tendency towards change and development on the part of the authors they admire (the same happened to Dickens, whose fans often implored him in his later years to return to the manner of *Pickwick* and *Chuzzlewit*); and even some of the professional critics of *Chance* noted with pleasure the signs of a revival of his earlier interests.

Contemporary reviewers were in general, as Norman Sherry says, 'ecstatic'. Words like 'wizardry' and 'entrancement' were bandied about, Conrad was referred to as 'one of the most gifted and original writers of our time', and this was called 'the best of his books'. In a curious sitting-on-the-fence assessment, Robert Lynd, a popular reviewer, declared it 'a book of magical genius' and 'one of the most original and fascinating of novels', but also suggested that its oblique method would lead many readers to find it 'tedious' (*Daily News*, 15 January 1914). A similarly mixed response was registered in his private journal by Arnold Bennett, who found the book 'discouraging' for a professional writer 'because he damn well knows he can't write as well as this', but also found the treatment at times 'so minute as to be unconvincing'. A little later Henry James described Conrad as 'a votary of the way to do a thing that shall make it undergo most doing'; his essay, reprinted in *Notes on Novelists* (1931), was (in Conrad's words) 'the *only time* a criticism affected me painfully'.

Moral isolation is again the theme of *Chance* – a characteristic that has led critics to link it both with *Under Western Eyes*, which precedes it, and with *Victory*, which follows it. Just as Heyst and Lena in the latter novel seek refuge on an island that, initially at least, recalls Eden, Flora and Anthony on the *Ferndale* are 'outside all conventions' like 'the first man and the first woman'. But evil, in the person of Jones and his companions, enters Heyst's paradisal retreat, and *Chance* follows a similar pattern: as C. B. Cox says in his comparison of the two novels, in both of them 'the heroes are defeated by wayward chance' and both are 'more successful in depicting moral isolation than in realizing a viable alternative'.

As a little later in *Victory*, the influence of Dickens is strongly felt in *Chance* – indeed, it can be argued that the same Dickens novel, *Dombey and Son*, is a potent presence. Flora de Barral, whose very name is close to that of Florence Dombey, is a motherless girl whose business-man father suffers a collapse of his financial empire, and there are echoes of scenes and settings (Brighton, for example, plays a part in both novels).

In one respect the popular success of *Chance* is surprising, since the novel is far from being an easy read on account of a mode of narration that has been variously described as cumbersome and absurd. Marlow, who tells the story to the narrator, himself reports much of it at second or third hand. The general verdict has been that the gain in subtlety or dramatic effectiveness is so slight as hardly to justify such lengths of elaboration. Leavis admits his 'irritation' with Marlow, and Cox points out that this is not the Marlow of *Lord Jim* or *Heart of Darkness* but a changed Marlow: 'Marlow appears to have lost some of the respect for human nature which characterizes his namesake in [the earlier books].

1. Conrad as a child (1863).
   The Mansell Collection.

2. Conrad's father,
   Apollo
   Korzeniowski
   in 1862.
   *The Beinecke Rare
   Book and Manuscript
   Library, Yale University.*

3. Conrad in 1874 (aged
   about 16).
   The Mansell Collection

4. Conrad in 1883
   (aged 25).
   *The National Library of
   Warsaw.*

5. Conrad in 1896
(aged about 38).
*The Beinecke Rare Book
and Manuscript Library,
Yale University.*

6. Conrad in 1912 (aged about 54).
The Estate of John Conrad.   Photo by William Cadby.

7. Conrad in 1923 (aged about 65).
The Estate of John Conrad.   Photo by T. and R. Annan and Sons.

8. Bust of Conrad by Jacob Epstein.
The Mansell Collection.

9. Portrait of Conrad by Walter Tittle.
The Mansell Collection.

10. 'Somewhere in the Pacific': Caricature of Conrad by Max Beerbohm, 1920.
by kind permission of Sir Rupert Hart-Davis/Mrs Eva Reichmann.

11. Edward Garnrett.
by kind permission of Richard Garnett.

12. R. B. Cunninghame Graham (etching by William Strang, 1898).
The Mansell Collection.

13. Jessie George in 1893.
University of Texas Library.

14. Marguerite Poradowska.
Duke University Library, North Carolina (the Virginia Grey Fund).

15. The Torrens.
The National Maritime Museum.

16. The Roi des Belges.
Norman Sherry.

His misogyny is simply unpleasant'. Walter Allen makes a similar
point in somewhat different terms in his *The English Novel* (1954):

> Marlow is admittedly a *persona* for Conrad himself; but there are
> times, as in *Heart of Darkness* and *Lord Jim*, when he is more than
> a *persona*; a character in his own right involved in the action and
> changed by it. Later, in *Chance*, he is scarcely involved and
> certainly not changed. Then he is a device and nothing more.

More generally, Allen observes that Conrad 'did his finest work
when he dispensed with [Marlow] and relied for the expression of
his point of view on other means. For Marlow has one fatal defect:
he talks too much and sometimes in the wrong way'.

On the evaluation of this novel as a whole there is no consensus.
For Leavis it is 'a remarkable novel', but others have seen it as
symptomatic of Conrad's decline in his later years. Douglas
Hewitt, for instance, regards it as a failure, and Jocelyn Baines
describes it as 'certainly one of Conrad's most imperfect novels'.

VICTORY

Begun in May 1912, *Victory* was originally conceived as a short story but outgrew this initial conception – an experience common enough with Conrad, who worked on it intermittently for some two years and completed it by the end of June 1914. The surviving manuscript shows that it was very extensively revised and that some of Conrad's original notions underwent radical transformation (see Frederick R. Karl, *Joseph Conrad: The Three Lives*, pp. 765–7). It was serialized in *Munsey's Magazine* (New York) in February 1915 and in the London *Star* from 24 August to 9 November 1915. Volume publication in New York was in March 1915 (10 000 copies) and in London in the following September (8000 copies); the size of these editions, compared with the 3000 copies each of *Under Western Eyes* and *Chance* only a few years earlier, indicates that its commercial prospects benefited from the success of *Chance*.

Its critical reception was favourable, and Norman Sherry refers to a 'chorus of praise'. As Sherry also points out, some reviewers recognized that it was different in kind from Conrad's earlier novels in being allegorical rather than realistic: one reviewer spoke of the encounter of the protagonist and the villains as resembling 'a struggle between the spiritual powers of the universe temporarily incarnate in a little group of human beings on a lonely Pacific island' (*Scotsman*, 27 September 1915), while another declared that the issue was 'as clear as in a Mystery play – the conflict between the forces of darkness and of light' (*Nation*, 2 October 1915). The latter comparison is echoed by a later critic, M. C. Bradbrook, who writes in *Joseph Conrad: Poland's English Genius* that 'The characters are drastically simplified, and take on something of the quality of figures in a morality play.' This generic question is a point of considerable critical importance, since critics who have persisted in regarding *Victory* as cast in a mode of realism have sometimes found it excessively schematic

114

and have found some of its characters (especially its heroine and its desperadoes) unconvincingly thin or melodramatic.

The hero, Axel Heyst (at first named Berg in Conrad's manuscript), has been deeply influenced by the sceptical and somewhat aristocratic philosophy of his father: the elder Heyst's stance has been to cultivate an aloofness from the involvements and entanglements of human relationships, and the fact that even on his island retreat of Samburan the younger Heyst has his father's portrait and his books suggests that he has adopted this outlook as a model for his own life. As he says later, he has sought to make his life 'a masterpiece of aloofness'. However, like Jim in *Lord Jim* and Razumov in *Under Western Eyes*, he is (in his own phrase) 'tempted into action' and thus becomes unavoidably, and in the end tragically, involved with the world that he has sought to exclude both geographically and spiritually. As F. R. Leavis says, the subject-matter of the novel is Heyst's 'unwilling involvements and their consequences'.

When he finds that the obnoxious Mrs Zangiacomo is evidently bullying as well as exploiting the pathetic Lena, he is 'surprised into a sympathetic start': his conditioning has not been complete enough to safeguard him from this human virtue or weakness. Carrying her off to his island, he believes that 'Nothing can break in on us here'. But a trio of assorted villains turns up, impelled by the conviction that he has a hidden treasure (as, in a metaphorical sense, he has): as one of them remarks, ' "I am the world itself, come to pay you a visit." ' They are, however, less the world than the evil that it is in the world; and the repetitive imagery associated with them continually stresses their inhumanity (another character, Schomberg, thinks of them as 'a spectre, a cat, an ape'). If Heyst and Lena stand for different aspects of humanity – he for its intellectual and philosophical aspirations, however misguided, she for its power of loving and suffering – they represent between them a subhuman lust, violence and destructiveness. As in a morality play, the forces of light and darkness are marshalled against each other.

The depiction of the three villains goes far to justify Baines' verdict that *Victory* is 'an essentially non-realistic book'. Mr Jones, tall and preternaturally emaciated, is compared to a corpse, a death's head, a ghost and a spirit; he speaks with 'a ghostly voice' and walks through the tall tropical grass 'almost as slender as a stalk of grass himself', representing in fact a kind of death-in-life and an almost disembodied malignity. Ricardo, on the other hand, is animalistic and repeatedly compared to a 'beast of prey', specifically a large cat or tiger: his moustaches stir 'in an odd, feline manner'; when he gets up it is 'with a snarl and a stretch'; at one point he is described as 'purring and spitting'; and in the powerful scene in which he attacks Lena his behaviour is 'feral'. He even has a knife strapped to his leg as a counterpart to the feline claws; and life for him, we learn, is a matter of 'a particularly active warfare' – the opposite of the quietism and withdrawal that Heyst has aspired to. The third of them, Pedro, is compared at different times to an ape (he has wide nostrils and 'thick brown hairy paws of simian aspect'), a bear (with 'fangs' and 'little bear's eyes'), and a dog: if Ricardo represents cunning, combined with savage lust, Pedro's is the mindless brute force of 'a bulky animal'.

The struggle between the two sides on the island resolves itself into Lena's attempt to save Heyst; and the climax is reached with her dying conviction that she has both saved him and won his love. This is Lena's 'victory' – but it is difficult to see the novel's title as other than ironic, for her conviction is groundless, Heyst is unable to respond to her sacrifice with spontaneous words of love; and, realizing that his lack of 'trust in life' and the capacity to love have been a fundamental error, he commits suicide. Leavis's interpretation that the victory is Heyst's, 'a victory over scepticism, a victory of life', undiminished by his death, is persuasively rejected by Baines, who sees the 'victory' as Lena's, and bitterly ironic ('though absolutely real to her' it 'has no objective reality'). The choice here is between an optimistic affirmation of the validity of Heyst's 'progressive self-discovery' (in Leavis's phrase), with the emphasis on that 'trust in life' of which Heyst speaks at the end, and a pessimistic acceptance that Lena's sacrifice has been in vain and her dying belief ('I've saved you!') groundless.

The 'Author's Note' of 1920, which replaced an earlier note, refers to the real-life prototypes of the three villains. A significant source of a different kind has been convincingly argued by K. H. Gatch (*Studies in Philology*, XLVIII, 1951), who has shown that Conrad's novel bears many similarities to Villiers de l'Isle Adam's drama *Axël*, in which the protagonist, like Heyst, withdraws from the world to a lonely spot, is invaded by a representative of the outside world in quest of supposed treasure, and ends by committing suicide.

Critical assessments of *Victory* have been decidedly mixed, 'excellent in parts' being a common verdict. Thus, Baines judges the characterization of Heyst an outstanding success ('perhaps the most interesting, and certainly the most complex, character that Conrad created'), but finds him 'the only three-dimensional character in the book', while for Cox the novel 'includes some of the best and worst of Conrad's writing'. Guerard has hardly a good word to say for it, dismissing it as 'Conrad for the high schools and the motion pictures' (evidently a response to its somewhat schematic moral pattern); Leavis, on the other hand, places it 'among those of Conrad's works which deserve to be current as representing his claim to classical standing'. All in all, Karl's observation that it is 'the most controversial of Conrad's novels' seems to be justified.

Part of the problem seems to be that Conrad is working simultaneously in two modes or fictional genres: whereas Heyst represents the method of psychological realism, the three villains are grotesques and caricatures, and the insistent (to some tastes over-insistent) imagery used to evoke their bizarre presences is working in a non-realistic mode of poetic symbolism. The effect is rather as if, say, Dickens and George Eliot had collaborated on a novel; and indeed the influence of Dickens – often to be felt in Conrad's work (*The Secret Agent* is another case in point) – is a potent one in *Victory*. Conrad read Dickens in Polish as a child and must have caught some of the enthusiasm of his father, who translated *Hard Times* into Polish; as an established writer, in *A Personal Record* and elsewhere, he made no secret of his continuing admiration. In *Victory* we encounter a phenomenon similar to that found in, for instance, *The Old Curiosity Shop*, where such characters as Quilp and Dick Swiveller exist on different fictional planes but nevertheless come face to face within a single work. Baines has gone so far as to describe *Victory* as 'an essentially non-realistic book'; and although this may be less true of some elements than of others, it points the way towards a mode of reading and interpretation that takes account of the distinctive nature of this novel. (On Conrad and Dickens, see F. R. Karl, *Notes & Queries*, ccii, 1957; on Dickensian elements in *Victory*, see Norman Page, *Conradiana*, v, 1973.) Karl's comment on the tendency of Conrad's extensive manuscript revisions is relevant to this point:

. . . in the manuscript Conrad attempted a far greater degree of realism than he felt was suitable in his final version. The manuscript fills out characters, situations, and scenes which in the book are approached more obliquely and suggestively. Throughout his revisions, after the manuscript was complete, Conrad moved towards a more symbolic presence.

THE SHADOW-LINE

As Frederick R. Karl has pointed out in his biography of Conrad, after *Victory*, completed in 1914 and published in the following year, 'all of Conrad's work was an extension of *A Personal Record*' – that is to say, it was either explicitly offered as reminiscences or, in the case of the novels and short stories, was fictionalized autobiography, a reliving and reshaping of his own earlier experiences. Karl adds that 'The unevenness of this work resulted chiefly from Conrad's inability to turn personal experience into creative materials'; but perhaps it would be more accurate to say that this was an ability that Conrad could not consistently sustain. Certainly in *The Shadow-Line* the transformation is masterly, and the work has elicited the highest praise from some of Conrad's critics. He himself made no secret of its origins: a letter to John Quinn describes it as 'a sort of autobiography'; one to Pinker goes further in saying that it is 'not a story really but exact autobiography'; and that last phrase is also used in a letter to Sidney Colvin ('the whole thing is exact autobiography'), where he adds that he 'always meant to do it'.

Its origins go back a full generation to 1888, when Conrad quitted the *Vidar* and, at a loose end in Singapore, was unexpectedly given the command of the *Otago* and went forthwith to Bangkok to take up his first command. He retained the Gulf of Siam as his setting in the story and stayed close to the events and even the names of those involved in his own experiences (he states in the letter to Colvin that Giles, based on a Captain Patterson, is 'the only name I've changed', but it appears that the prototype of Burns was called Born). There are strong resemblances between *The Shadow-Line* and Conrad's slightly earlier story 'The Secret Sharer', and the comparison has often been made. When the young captain enters his cabin for the first time and, sitting in the chair in which so many of his predecessors ('a dynasty') have sat, watches himself reflected in the mirror 'both as if he were myself and somebody else', we seem to draw very close to the theme of

119

'The Secret Sharer'; but the later work is without the portentousness and over-insistence of that story.

Conrad began work on *The Shadow-Line* early in 1915 and finished it by the end of that year. It is thus a wartime story, and its dedication to Borys Conrad, who was serving in the armed forces, as well as to the other young men of his generation, brings together the experiences of the two generations of father and son. It was serialized in the *English Review* from September 1916 to March 1917 and in the *Metropolitan* (New York) in October 1916, and appeared in volume form in March 1917. (At some 40 000 words it is considerably shorter than the normal novel-length, but nevertheless achieved separate volume-publication.) Following the success of *Chance* and *Victory*, the reviews were generally favourable, though there was some tendency to equate its brevity with slightness. Writing in the *Sphere* (14 April 1917), the well-known critic Clement Shorter took the opportunity to note that Conrad had now 'arrived' as a popular as well as a critically esteemed writer:

> . . . with his eighteenth book, *Victory*, Mr Conrad became not only one of the favourite novelists of the elect but one of the favourite novelists of the many.

An anonymous reviewer in the *Nation* (24 March 1917) described the book as 'written at Mr Conrad's fullest imaginative stretch'. A review in the *Bookman* (June 1917), while judging it 'scarcely one of Mr Conrad's big achievements', presumably on the grounds of its brevity, conceded that it was 'distinguished by that unmistakable air of vraisemblance in narrative and dialogue alike which is one of the most attractive notes of its author's manner'. Conrad himself was exasperated by the numerous attempts to detect a supernatural element in the story; suggestions that at various points it echoes Coleridge's 'The Ancient Mariner' were particularly common.

The title is explicated both in the dedication and in the story itself: '. . . the time, too, goes on – till one perceives ahead a shadow-line warning one that the region of early youth, too, must be left behind'. Conrad was thirty when he took command of the *Otago* – an age that has seemed to many people a landmark in their existence; and as F. R. Leavis says in his fine essay on *The Shadow-Line* in *Anna Karenina and Other Essays* (1967), 'The ship and the command are, for the young Captain, a symbol and a test: the experience in the Gulf of Siam is an ordeal, a kind of *rite de passage*.' When the new captain sees his ship for the first time, his 'feeling of life-emptiness' or failure to discover any urgent purpose in life is suddenly replaced by 'a flow of joyous emotion', and that joy is not destroyed by the bitter difficulties with which he is soon confronted.

Albert Guerard has argued that the story is weak in its opening sections, which move sluggishly and uncertainly as if the raw material of remembered experience has been inadequately reshaped into art. This view is disputed by Ian Watt ('Joseph Conrad: Alienation and Commitment', in *The English Mind*, ed. Hugh Sykes Davies & George Watson [Cambridge, 1964]), who sees this effect as a deliberate contrast to what follows, as the young man moves from the shore world of the Officers' Home, with its aimless derelicts, to the ship and the voyage. Two critics already cited, Cox and Leavis, show another significant difference of interpretation. For Cox, although this is 'Conrad's last masterpiece', it is a simpler, less resonant work than 'The Secret Sharer': whereas that is 'typical of Conrad's modernism' and 'a story of questioning and uncertainty about the grounds of being and action', *The Shadow-Line* is 'comparatively straightforward' and 'ends with the test satisfactorily completed'. For Leavis, on the other hand, ' "The Secret Sharer" . . . undertakes much less than *The Shadow-Line* does', and the latter is 'a profound work, and complex in its profundity'.

THE ARROW OF GOLD

Conrad wrote (or, largely, dictated) this novel quite rapidly: composition occupied less than a year, and it was finished on 4 June 1918. It was serialized in *Lloyd's Magazine* from December 1918 to June 1920, and appeared in volume form in London and New York in 1919. The dedication is to Richard Curle. To some extent *The Arrow of Gold* is a reworking of Conrad's unfinished novel *The Sisters* (published posthumously), the heroine of which shares a name and much else with the heroine of the later book. Conrad also reworked material that had appeared in the penultimate chapter ('The "Tremolino" ') of *The Mirror of the Sea*, though a significant difference between the two versions is aptly noted by Frederick Karl: 'The novel is the obverse of the *'Tremolino'* in *The Mirror of the Sea*, as if additional retrospect had bleached out the adventure and brought into relief the romance'.

The action of the novel is set in the 1870s, some forty years earlier than the date of composition – in other words, in the period of Conrad's own youth. He had been in Marseilles, where the action takes place, in 1877–8, but the novel is set in 1875 – a more exciting moment in history, since at that time the Carlist war was still in progress and there was still some possibility that the Pretender would obtain the throne. (Civil war over the Carlist question in Spain had been recommenced in 1870 by Don Carlos, grandson of the original claimant to the throne; he suffered military defeats in 1872 and 1874, and in 1876 was forced to seek exile in France.)

The novel has an important autobiographical basis, and its protagonist, Monsieur George, has much in common with the young Conrad, who was known in Marseilles as 'Monsieur Georges'. The personal element ought not, however, to be exaggerated: this is, after all, fiction and not autobiography, and nostalgic memory and a kind of retrospective wish-fulfilment had a powerful effect on Conrad's recreation of the past. As Karl observes, 'Over all is an aura of his reading and imagination, not of reality'. Conrad wrote in a letter (16 January 1921) that his correspondent's 'surmise that Mr George of the Arrow of Gold is in a sense myself is just', but due weight needs to be given to that saving phrase 'in a sense' as well as to the fact that Conrad was notoriously unreliable in recalling details of his own past. In this wartime book, another relevant biographical circumstance is Borys Conrad's war service: his father was not only recreating and reshaping his own distant past, but reliving his adventurous youth through the experiences and dangers to which his son was exposed.

The serious weaknesses of this novel have been generally recognized: it is slow-moving and portentous, and the principal characters never really come to life. Karl's diagnosis is that these weaknesses stem from Conrad's failure to transform 'life' into 'art':

> . . . Conrad caught himself between conflicting demands. Using art to disguise life, he never used it sufficiently, and using life as the basis of art, he was insufficiently honest with himself.

This antithesis perhaps oversimplifies the situation, however, since 'life' in this instance was partly public history, partly private history more or less accurately recalled, and partly unfulfilled dream. There seem to be dangers, too, in Karl's further comment that 'because *Arrow* strains for its effects, we are tempted to view it as biography, precisely because it fails as art'. An unsatisfactory novel cannot be assumed to be a satisfactory autobiography, and the temptation ought to be resisted. Some have taken the view that the weakness of this novel is a symptom of the general decline of Conrad's powers in his later years. Baines, however, rejects this on the grounds that a later novel, *The Rover*, is markedly superior, and attributes the shortcomings of *The Arrow of Gold* to the fact that it was composed rapidly and with 'a lack of concentrated care'. Conrad himself seems to admit this in a letter of 31 December 1917 (quoted by Baines), where he speaks of the novel as being composed 'with groans and imprecations. . . . You can imagine what sort of stuff that is. No colour, no relief, no tonality, the thinnest possible squeaky bubble'. There is bitterness in his further comment that 'when I've finished with it, I shall go out and sell it in a market place for twenty times the money I had for the *Nigger*, thirty times the money I had for the *Mirror of the Sea*'.

His original plan involved narrating the story, wholly or in part, through a series of letters written by the protagonist to a woman he had known in his youth, the protagonist being a man of about Conrad's own age. As it stands, the form of the novel is a first-person narrative introduced by an editorial note describing the narrative as having been 'extracted from a pile of manuscript', and concluding with another note stating that 'The narrative of our man goes on for some six months more . . .' and giving an account of the loss of the 'arrow of gold', the piece of jewellery that is a recurring symbol throughout the book. This structure gives the novel its subtitle, 'A Story between Two Notes'.

A fatal weakness at the heart of the novel is that, though this is primarily a love story, the hero's passion for Rita is presented as a somewhat abstract affair. As for Rita herself, even though Conrad claimed that he was offering a 'study of a woman' (letter of 18 February 1918), she remains no more than a shadow. The unrealized nature of the situations is often betrayed by the heavily abstract quality of Conrad's language:

> . . . she was but the principle of life charged with fatality. Her form was only a mirage of desire decoying one step by step into despair.

Elsewhere he writes that 'The woman was a mere chaos of sensations and vitality' – but sensations and vitality are precisely what, as a fictional creation, Rita lacks. The hero speaks in a jargon characteristic of the bad Conrad, and is greatly addicted to negative epithets that gesture towards large meanings ('an inconceivable intimacy', 'a great, glowing, indeterminate tenderness'); but his emotions, like the characters and situations of the novel, remains curiously unreal. At times Conrad comes close to self-parody:

> It was as if I had reached the ultimate wisdom beyond all dreams and all passions. She was That which is to be Contemplated to all Infinity.

One would like to be able to believe that the narrator is here exposing his former self to some ironic self-mockery, as when David Copperfield reflects wryly on his own youthful follies; but the tone of the book as a whole does not justify such a charitable interpretation.

Abstraction, inflation, cliché: these are the recurrent weaknesses of Conrad's style in this late novel. The heroine does not simply smile, she smiles 'with an inscrutable smile that a great painter might have put on the face of some symbolic figure for the speculation and wonder of many generations'; and when she laughs it is with a 'deep contralto laugh . . . profoundly moving by the mere purity of the sound'. But at such moments Conrad is like an incompetent confidence trickster trying to impose on an audience that is unprepared to be duped: no reader is likely to be taken in by such phrases as 'profoundly moving', which lay claim to a meaning they do not really possess. Sometimes the writing lapses into the absurd: at one point the hero 'hissed forcibly the warning "Perfect immobility" ' (the reader might care to try hissing that stilted phrase in either English or French), and elsewhere the heroine gives what is quaintly described as an 'enigmatic, under the eyebrows glance'.

Another approach to a diagnosis of the pervasive weakness of this novel is to point out that there is in it almost nothing about *work*, the theme that prompted most of Conrad's best writing. The hero describes himself at one point as ' "a very good gun-runner" ', but we see almost nothing of his gun-running or any other activity. This absence becomes fully explicit only on the final pages of the novel, where a character observes:

You know that this world is not a world for lovers, not even for such lovers as you two. . . . No, a world of lovers would be impossible. It would be a mere ruin of lives that seem to be meant for something else . . .

and the same character (Mills) tells the hero on the last page of the book that he will ' "always have your . . . other love – you pig-headed enthusiast of the sea'. When Conrad wrote of that 'other love' he was at his best, but in the *Arrow* he was almost at his worst. The novel might just conceivably have made a workable short story, but its falsity and its *longueurs* make it a novel that few readers will be impatient to return to. Conrad had written to Cunninghame Graham on 8 February 1899 in connection with *Heart of Darkness*, '. . . you must remember that I don't start with an abstract notion. I start with definite images and as their rendering is true some little effect is produced'. The trouble with *The Arrow of Gold* is that, in spite of the personal origins of the story, the 'definite images' seem to have been absent or at least impossibly faint, and the book both begins and ends on the level of 'an abstract notion'.

Contemporary reception of the novel was mixed (Sherry describes it as 'an uncertain press'). Apparently hypnotised by Conrad's successes earlier in the decade and his new-found fame, a few reviewers bestowed praise on it that makes one gasp: Sir Sidney Colvin, for instance, described it as 'a study of a woman's heart and mystery scarcely to be surpassed in literature' (*Observer*, 24 August 1919), and an anonymous reviewer in the *Morning Post* (6 August 1919) found it 'an extraordinarily fascinating work'. Others were less enthusiastic, but it was generally treated with respect, and Sherry notes that 'With the publication of *The Arrow of Gold*, Conrad became the grand old man of letters, taking over the mantle of Thomas Hardy' – an accolade explicitly bestowed by the *New Statesman* (16 August 1919), whose reviewer even-handedly noted that 'a new novel by Mr Conrad is an "event" – even if, as in the present case, the new book is something of a disappointment'.

THE RESCUE

Completed on 25 May 1919, this was Conrad's most protracted
literary undertaking, having been begun some twenty-three years
earlier at the time of his marriage and after laying aside the
unfinished novel *The Sisters*. Over the years Conrad had worked at
it intermittently and had several times promised its impending
completion – for example, in 1898, while working on *Lord Jim*, he
actually undertook to deliver the manuscript of *The Rescue*
(originally titled *The Rescuer: a Tale of Narrow Waters*) for publication in the *Illustrated London News*, and the editor, Clement Shorter,
made his plans to begin serialization in October of that year; and
at the end of 1902 Conrad told another publisher, Blackwood,
that he expected to finish it within a few months, though he
admitted that it was going 'slowly, very slowly'.

It was serialized in *Land and Water* from 30 January to 31 July
1919, and in the New York magazine *Romance* from November
1919 to May 1920. As the dates of English serialization indicate, it
was not completed until a fairly late stage of the serial run.
Volume publication, with the subtitle *A Romance of the Shallows*,
followed in 1920. The dedication is to Frederic Courtland
Penfield, the United States Ambassador to Vienna who had
helped the Conrads to escape from Austria after they had been
trapped on the Continent by the outbreak of war in 1914. The text
was extensively revised between serialization and volume publication, and incorporates suggestions made by Garnett.

The Rescue returns to the world of Conrad's earliest novels,
Almayer's Folly and *An Outcast of the Islands*; and its protagonist had
already appeared in the latter novel. The Lingard of *The Rescue* is
younger than the Lingard of *An Outcast*, just as *An Outcast* had
depicted an earlier phase of his life than appears in *Almayer's Folly*;
thus the three novels form, in Frederick R. Karl's apt phrase, 'a
special kind of trilogy in reverse chronological order'. In a letter of
15 February 1919, Conrad wrote: 'It may well be that [*The Rescue*]
. . . will remain the swan song of Romance as a literary art'.

Certainly its themes and techniques are those to which he had been favourably disposed throughout his career. About its success there have been wide differences of opinion. Baines finds it, though 'unashamedly romantic', 'a work of considerable merit'; he praises the depiction of Lingard as hero ('although a legitimately romantic figure he is presented in a wholly adult manner and is involved in an adult situation') and the 'firm moral pivot' of the story: 'The interest of the action hinges on the conflict in Lingard's mind between his pledge to Hassim and his obligation to save the lives of the people from the stranded yacht'. Baines also finds Mrs Travers, with whom Lingard falls in love, 'one of Conrad's few convincing female portraits'. Karl, on the other hand, finds that 'it contains everything good and bad in his work' but is on the whole 'sluggish and only infrequently engages the mind seriously'; and he can see in the hero Lingard only 'the emotions of a little boy . . . too weak emotionally and too headstrong in love to sustain nearly five hundred pages of romantic prose'. Karl concedes that 'thematically and structurally it provides an excellent résumé of Conrad's entire career'.

Conrad's reputation by this time can be estimated from the fact that 20 000 copies of the first edition were printed. Contemporary reviewers were enthusiastic and even fulsome: one found the novel 'so massive, so profound, so beautiful' (*Sketch*, 21 July 1920), while another judged it Conrad's masterpiece (*Glasgow Evening News*, 5 August 1920). Some made the shrewd point that Conrad had come a long way since the early stories in which women are either entirely absent or present in only a minor role: as Rose Macaulay wrote (*Time and Tide*, 9 July 1920), 'Mr Conrad's sure touch on men always a little fails him with women.' Norman Sherry has made the point that both *The Arrow of Gold* and *The Rescue* are 'essentially tales of love-bewitched men'. An interesting review in the *Times Literary Supplement* (1 July 1920), which seems to be by Virginia Woolf, discusses Conrad as a romantic writer and reaches the conclusion that in this novel he 'has attempted a romantic theme and in the middle his belief in romance has failed him' – a weakness no doubt attributable to the peculiar circumstances of its composition.

THE ROVER

The Rover, Conrad's last completed novel, is, like *Suspense*, a historical novel set in the Napoleonic period. It may have taken its origins in the wide reading that Conrad undertook when he was working on *Suspense*, work on which was interrupted by the composition of the other novel.

A date on the manuscript indicates that work on *The Rover* began early in October 1921. As so often with Conrad, the scale of the original conception was considerably more modest than the eventual outcome: it was envisaged as a story of about 12 000 words. Progress was slow, and by December only some 5500 words had been written; at the same time, the dimensions of the tale were expanding, Conrad remarking to Pinker on 19 December that he intended to 'make that tale as long as possible, within the long short-story limits'. At this stage he planned to publish it in a volume that also included 'Prince Roman', which had been published ten years earlier but in the event remained uncollected until after Conrad's death. In the early months of 1922 Conrad suffered periods of illness, but work on *The Rover* continued, portions of it being dictated. Progress was still slow, and by late April only the first six chapters had been dispatched to Pinker. Then things improved, and in May and June Conrad composed ten chapters, or about two-thirds of the book. It was completed on 27 June, and nearly three further weeks were spent on revision and expansion. Composition was still a painful business for Conrad, and he told Garnett on 24 May that he had never been 'so exasperated with anything I have had to do'.

The novel was published on 3 December (1 December in New York), with a dedication to G. Jean-Aubry. Conrad's status as a best-seller by this stage in his career may be measured by the size of the British edition, which was 40 000 copies. Sales were very good, its American success no doubt being helped (as Najder points out) by the recent sale in New York of Quinn's collection of Conrad's manuscripts, which had attracted widespread publicity. Najder writes:

The reception given *The Rover* was, all in all, the reverse of how Conrad's books had been received twenty-five or fifteen years earlier: now popular acclaim and sales were high, while the voices of the reviewers were cool and censorious.

This last statement calls for some qualification, however. It is true that Raymond Mortimer in the *New Statesman* (15 December 1923) judged it 'downright bad' and remarked acidly that 'contact with [Conrad's] mind does not seem to me a delight in itself'; that Leonard Woolf (*Nation and Athenaeum*, 8 December 1923) described it as 'melodramatic'; that the *Glasgow Evening News* (6 December 1923) found it 'a disappointment'; and that a particularly hostile reviewer in the *New York Tribune* (4 December 1923) declared that it was 'the worst he ever wrote' and 'probably an awful punk book' ('punk' in those far-off days apparently meaning 'worthless' or 'inferior'). But this was only one side of the picture, for the *Manchester Guardian* praised the narrative as 'as fast and as bare as the wind' (3 December 1923), and the *Times Literary Supplement* (6 December 1923) similarly approved of the narrative economy: 'Mr Conrad, certainly, has written greater things than this; but among his recent books it stands out for the speed of movement, and not less for the impress of its truth to human nature'. As Norman Sherry points out, in the views of some critics at least Conrad had fulfilled the 'secret desire to achieve a feat of artistic brevity' of which he speaks to Garnett in a letter of 4 December 1923.

Peyrol, the protagonist, is an old man who has been a master gunner in the French Navy. Following an 'instinct of rest', he has settled in a lonely inn near Toulon. Jean-Aubry aptly draws attention to the significance of Conrad's portrayal, near the end of his life, of an elderly sailor whose only desire is for rest; and it is touching to reflect that the epigraph of the novel, two lines from Spenser, were soon to be used again on Conrad's tombstone. Najder notes that

> this was the only book written in the closing years of his life which engaged many of the author's deepest sentiments: his nostalgia for the Mediterranean, his dislike of revolution, and his acquired English patriotism which is in constant contrast to the austere and yet spontaneous attachment to man's native soil shown by the novel's French hero.

Conrad himself described the book to Garnett (letter of 21 November 1923) as 'a thing of sentiment – of many sentiments'. While assuredly a minor novel, it has not been unadmired, Baines for instance regarding it as 'a worthy swansong' and suggesting that 'the writing shows no decline in power'.

SUSPENSE

Suspense remained unfinished at Conrad's death, some 80 000 words existing of what was evidently to have been a long novel. It was serialized in the *Saturday Review of Literature* from 27 June to 12 August 1925, and published in volume form in September of the same year.

Subtitled *A Napoleonic Novel*, *Suspense* occupied Conrad on and off for about twenty years. In *Joseph Conrad: The Making of a Novelist* (1940), John D. Gordan reminds us that, even though Conrad based so much of his fiction on first-hand experience, he also drew heavily on printed sources, and many episodes in his novels and stories are based on his reading. For *Suspense* he pursued his researches into the Napoleonic period, and during some of the rather rare holidays he took from writing – for instance, in Capri in 1905, in Montpellier in 1907, and in Corsica early in 1921 – he read histories and memoirs, as well as seeking out material in the British Museum. (The short story 'The Warrior's Soul' was a minor offshoot of these researches, and the novel *The Rover* a more substantial byproduct.) An important source, from which Conrad seems to have derived his plot, was the *Memoirs* of the Comtesse de Boigne (see *Times Literary Supplement*, 25 February 1926, and *Modern Language Notes*, 1935).

Conrad told Hueffer that the story was to end with Napoleon's departure from Elba; apart from this, his intentions for the unwritten portion are unknown. In a letter to his agent Pinker on 3 February 1924, a few months before his death, he described it as 'a biggish thing' and predicted that those who had found *The Rover* 'rather slight' would 'find weight and body enough in what's coming'. When the book appeared, Garnett responded to an adverse review in the *New Statesman* (26 September 1925), in which the reviewer had declared that it 'does not come to life at all', by declaring that it was 'a pure work of art' and 'the most mature of all Conrad's works' (*Weekly Westminster*, 10 October 1925). The modern reader's verdict is likely to fall somewhere between these extremes: while far from unreadable, *Suspense* moves so slowly as hardly to justify its title, and even in a complete state there is no reason to believe that it would have been a major achievement or a significant reversal of the creative decline of Conrad's last years. An interesting review that maintains a careful balancing-act between praise and blame is that by Leonard Woolf (*Nation & Athenaeum*, 3 October 1925), reprinted in *Critical Heritage*. Woolf found in it 'many of Conrad's great merits' and judged the characters 'typically Conradian', but was left, 'despite its solidity and seriousness', with 'a strong feeling of emptiness and hollowness'. He expanded this observation into a general comment on the later Conrad:

> . . . I had the feeling which one gets on cracking a fine, shining, new walnut, which has just dropped from the tree, only to find that it has nothing inside it. Most of the later Conrads give one this feeling. They are splendid shells, magnificent façades, admirable forms, but there is no life in them.

Woolf's metaphor, and his judgment, recall an oft-quoted and much-debated passage in E. M. Forster's 'Joseph Conrad: A Note', written a few years earlier (1920) and later reprinted in his *Abinger Harvest* (the occasion was a review of *Notes on Life and Letters*):

> These essays do suggest that he is misty in the middle as well as at the edges, that the secret casket of his genius contains a vapour rather than a jewel; and that we need not try to write him down philosophically, because there is, in this particular direction, nothing to write. No creed, in fact. Only opinions, and the right to throw them overboard when facts make them look absurd. Opinions held under the semblance of eternity, girt with the sea, crowned with the stars, and therefore easily mistaken for a creed.

Much Conrad criticism in recent years, on the other hand, has involved an attempt to show that Conrad had a 'creed' and that it was central to the achievement of his fiction.

THE SISTERS

Conrad began *The Sisters* in the autumn of 1895, shortly after completing his second novel, *An Outcast of the Islands*. He worked on it for several months and by March 1896 had written about 10 000 words; then he abandoned it, apparently on the advice of Edward Garnett, and turned to the novel that later became *The Rescue*. On 23 March he wrote a whimsical letter to Garnett that addressed him as 'O Gentle and Murderous Spirit' and declared, 'You have killed my cherished aspiration'; and on 9 April he told Garnett: '*The Sisters* are laid aside'. Exactly why Conrad should have described it as a 'cherished aspiration', or why Garnett, who had obviously read what he had written, should have dissuaded him from continuing, is not quite clear. Perhaps the 'aspiration' was to show that he could write a work of fiction that did not depend for its interest on an exotic setting; and perhaps, as Baines surmises, Garnett 'felt that Conrad was not getting to grips with the story and was anxious to guide him back to a sphere which he really knew so that he could both develop his talent and at the same time have some likelihood of a popular success'.

The action of the novel was to have been set in Passy, the district of Paris in which Marguerite Poradowska lived. The hero is a young painter named Stephen who has come from the Ukraine and settled in Paris. A second line of action concerns a young girl Rita, who has left her Basque village to come to Paris. (The name Rita was later to be used in *The Arrow of Gold*.) Evidently the two were to meet; presumably they were to fall in love; and apparently the story was to end tragically. The rest, as Baines says, must be 'guesswork'. Baines also notes that the style of the fragment is in places 'bizarrely stilted and lifeless', and its abandonment is probably no great loss. *The Sisters* was published in 1928, four years after Conrad's death, with an introduction by Ford Madox Ford.

Short Stories

Much of Conrad's time and energy went into the writing of short stories for magazine publication, since he badly needed the relatively high remuneration that this mode of writing provided. Short story is an elastic term in the Conrad canon, embracing pieces that range from short and slight tales to novellas as lengthy and important as 'Heart of Darkness'. Nearly all were originally published in a great variety of British and American periodicals. Conrad collected twenty-five of his stories in a series of six volumes, and a further four stories were collected in a posthumous volume.

TALES OF UNREST

Conrad's first collection of short stories was published by Fisher Unwin (London) on 4 April 1898 in an edition of 3000 copies. The dedication is to Adolf P. Krieger (see 'A Conrad Who's Who' above). The volume contains five stories, all but one of which had previously appeared in magazines, and its contents indicate Conrad's adoption of the short story as a medium at the time of his marriage. (A short story could generate income more rapidly, and sometimes more gratifyingly, than a novel: 'An Outpost of Progress', for instance, earned him fifty pounds, and 'The Idiots' forty-two pounds, from magazine editors – quite substantial sums at that time.) Norman Sherry notes that 'though *Tales of Unrest* was praised many reviewers pointed to the depressing nature of the tales'. An anonymous reviewer in the *Daily Telegraph* (9 April 1898) expressed the hope that in his next volume Conrad would 'choose more pleasant themes', and *Literature* (30 April 1898) deplored 'the imperturbable solemnity with which he piles the unnecessary on the commonplace'. However, at the beginning of 1899, Conrad was one of three writers (the others were Sidney Lee and Maurice Hewlett) awarded a prize by the weekly *Academy* for outstanding work produced during the previous year; in an article on 14 January the magazine stated that the award was made on the basis of *Tales of Unrest* and 'Youth', and observed that it was Conrad's 'achievement to have brought the East to our very doors'.

'Karain: a Memory' had originally appeared in the famous *Blackwood's Magazine* in November 1897. In his later 'Author's Note' Conrad states: 'it was my first contribution to *Blackwood's Magazine* and . . . led to my personal acquaintance with Mr William Blackwood' (the magazine was later to publish 'Youth', 'Heart of Darkness', and other work by Conrad). The same Note says that composition 'was begun on a sudden impulse only three days after I wrote the last line of the Nigger' – that is, in the second half of January 1897. It was sent to Unwin on 14 April, having been the cause of a good deal of trouble to its author, who seems to have had a poor opinion of it – he described it to Edward Garnett as 'magazine'ish'. Like his first two novels, it has a Malayan setting and its protagonist is haunted by the ghost of a man he has killed. As Baines comments, it 'oozes lush romanticism'. Ian Watt points out that in this story 'Conrad made his first full use of a participant narrator, an unnamed character who occasionally raised questions about the meanings and motives which the story involved'.

'The Idiots' was published in the *Savoy* in October 1896. It was written during Conrad's honeymoon earlier in that year (see under 1896 in 'A Conrad Chronology'), and was suggested by an actual encounter in Brittany. In a letter to Garnett it is described as 'a short story of Brittany Peasant life'. A lurid tale of murder and suicide, it nevertheless has a certain crude effectiveness, as well as being of some psychological interest in relation to Conrad's feelings about marriage and parenthood. It shows the influence of Maupassant and is summarily dismissed in the 'Author's Note' as 'an obviously derivative piece of work'.

The best story in the collection, 'An Outpost of Progress', appeared in *Cosmopolis* in June and July 1897, having also been written during Conrad's 1896 honeymoon in Brittany and sent to Garnett on 22 July of that year. His letter to Garnett says that he is 'pleased with it'; and on the same day he wrote to Unwin, 'It is a story of the Congo. There is no love interest in it . . .'. The 'Author's Note' describes it as 'the lightest part of the loot I carried off from Central Africa', and declares, 'it is true enough in its essentials'. Its relationship to the more substantial part of his African 'loot', 'Heart of Darkness', is a significant one: like that slightly later story, though in balder terms, its concern is with the moral disintegration of Europeans in tropical Africa. As Ian Watt says, it was at that stage in his career 'easily the most powerful and professional thing Conrad had yet done'.

'The Return' was written just after 'Karain' in 1897. The 'Author's Note' describes it as 'a left-handed production' and recalls how much it cost its author 'in sheer toil, in temper and in disillusion'. He was unable to place it with an editor (it was too long to publish undivided, and Conrad refused to allow it to be carved up), and there was no magazine publication. It represents, as Watt notes, a very different kind of fiction from Conrad's other productions of this period, and suggests that he was trying to 'break out of his rut': it is set not in Malaya or the Congo, but in 'fashionable London society', and explores the nature of a marriage relationship. Baines describes it as 'quite unlike any of Conrad's other stories, being a psychological drama without any important objective action'.

The last and shortest story in the volume, 'The Lagoon' had appeared in the top-drawer *Cornhill Magazine* in January 1897, and was another product of the previous year's honeymoon. Set in Malaya, and described in a letter to Garnett (5 August 1896) as 'very much Malay indeed', it returns to the world of Conrad's first two novels. He himself makes this point in his 'Author's Note' ('It . . . marks, in a manner of speaking, the end of my first phase'). The same note is misleading, however, in describing it as 'the first short story I ever wrote'.

In this story an unnamed white man is paddled by Malays via a narrow approach to a lagoon where a Malay friend lives in seclusion with his wife. The latter is dying, and the Malay tells the story of how he carried off the girl and, in his flight, abandoned the brother who was helping him and who met his death at the hands of the pursuers. The wife dies, and the man will now go to seek revenge for his brother's death.

Though a slight story, 'The Lagoon' contains some typical Conradian motifs. The Malay is an exile, living outside the world of action to which he can return only after the death of the woman for whose sake he has sacrificed his brother. His sudden, unpremeditated, irrevocable and bitterly regretted step in pushing off the boat and leaving his brother behind looks forward to Jim's jump from the *Patna*.

YOUTH: A NARRATIVE AND TWO OTHER STORIES

Conrad's second collection of stories was issued by the Edinburgh publishing firm of Blackwood's, publishers of the famous *Blackwood's Magazine* ('Maga') in which all three stories had previously appeared. 'Youth' had appeared in September 1898; 'Heart of Darkness' in February, March and April 1899 (as 'The Heart of Darkness'); and 'The End of the Tether' from July to December 1902. The volume appeared in November 1902 in an edition of 3150 copies. As Norman Sherry points out in *Critical Heritage*, reviewers tended to follow the lead of Edward Garnett, who praised the collection in an unsigned review in *Academy and Literature* (6 December 1902). In a letter to Garnett (22 December 1902), Conrad himself sardonically noted that enthusiastic reviewers echoed Garnett's very phrases:

> I notice the reviews as they come in since your article. Youth is an epic; that's settled. And the H. of D. is this and that and the other thing – they aren't so positive because in this case they aren't intelligent enough to catch on to your indications. But anyhow it's a high water mark . . .

(Garnett had referred to 'Youth' as 'a modern English epic of the Sea' and had praised 'Heart of Darkness' as 'the high-water mark of the author's talent'.) The size of the edition – it was, as J. D. Gordan notes in *Joseph Conrad: The Making of a Novelist*, 'the largest Conrad edition to date' – is a modest index of Conrad's growing reputation and also suggests that the reception of the stories when published in the magazine had been favourable. The volume, which Conrad referred to as 'the three-headed monster in the green cover', was dedicated to his wife.

'Youth', subtitled 'A Narrative', is also described as 'a feat of memory' and 'a record of experience'. (The manuscript shows that Conrad had considered, and rejected, 'A Voyage' as an alternative title.) It is closely based on his own ill-fated first voyage to the East on the *Palestine* in 1881–3 (see 'A Conrad Chronology' for details of the misfortunes and demise of the *Palestine*). Baines persuasively argues, however, that Jean-Aubry overstates the case in describing the story as 'precisely in every detail the story of the barque *Palestine*': for one thing, after the ship has been abandoned 'Marlow took as many days to get to land as Conrad in fact took hours'.

More recently, Najder has extended Baines' argument by showing that there are at least two major discrepancies between Conrad's experience and the account given in 'Youth'. In the first place,

> Conrad dramatized the accident, stretching it out in time and space and giving a different reason for parting with the towing steamer. In the tale the parting appears extremely risky; in reality, however, the disaster took place near shore. The boats did not steer for Java but toward the port of Muntok on Bangka island.

Moreover, there is a curious and revealing discrepancy relating to the composition of the crew:

> The crew Conrad extolled in 'Youth' was recruited from 'Liverpool hard cases' which not only could work with impressive self-discipline in critical moments, but also display surprising understanding for the beauty inherent in good sailsmanship. . . . But in fact there was not a single Liverpudlian on the *Palestine*. Five men came from Cornwall, one from Ireland, and the remainder were foreigners – an Australian, a Negro from the Antilles, a Dutchman, and a Norwegian.

In other words, this is fictionalized autobiography, like so much of Conrad's work – he offers no apology either for drawing heavily on personal experience or for modifying that experience consciously (in addition to whatever unconscious modifications may have been made by memory) in the process of transforming it into literature, and there is of course no reason at all why he should do so.

The story is one of Conrad's best-known and, much anthologized and used as a school text, it must have contributed to the popular conception of him as primarily if not exclusively a teller of tales about the sea. Its telling, however, shows a degree of sophistication and it is important as introducing for the first time the figure of Marlow as narrator-participant. As in 'Heart of Darkness' a little later, the story is set in a 'frame' situation: a group of five men, 'a director of companies, an accountant, a lawyer, Marlow, and myself', all sharing 'the strong bond of the sea', are sitting round a table after dinner; and to his fellow-diners Marlow tells 'the story, or rather the chronicle, of a voyage'. Marlow, as a mature and reflective man of the sea, has much in common with Conrad (he even has the same number of letters, and the same vowels, in his name); on the other hand, he is not Conrad and is seen objectively both by his creator and by the narrator ('myself') of the frame-story, who themselves may or may not be the same person. Conrad evidently liked the device so well that he revived it not only in 'Heart of Darkness' but in *Lord Jim* and *Chance*; moreover, he developed the role of Marlow, so that the Marlow of, for example, *Lord Jim* performs a considerably more complex and subtle function than his namesake of 'Youth'. No doubt Conrad was attracted by the opportunity of being able to comment and ruminate on the action without resorting to the intrusive interpolations of an omniscient narrator beloved by Thackeray, Trollope, and other Victorian novelists but distinctly out of favour by the turn of the century. The use of Marlow also enabled him to employ a more relaxed, informal, semi-colloquial style that may have acted as a corrective to the tendency to over-writing that had afflicted the lush prose of his earliest work.

In 'Youth' Conrad not only drew on the events and feelings of his own past but used (not for the first or last time) the names of actual men and an actual ship either thinly disguised or not disguised at all: the *Palestine* appears as the *Judea*, and the captain (Beard: see 'A Conrad Who's Who') and the mate (Mahon) both appear under their own names. In 'Heart of Darkness' he was to do the same, though in some important instances the relationship between fact and fiction in this story is more complex and more debatable (see the entries for Hodister and Klein in 'A Conrad Who's Who'). Again Conrad made no secret of the autobiographical origins, describing it as 'experience pushed a little (and only a little) beyond the actual facts of the case . . .' ('Author's Note'). For details of his experiences in the Congo on which the story is based, see 'A Conrad Chronology' under the date 1890.

'Heart of Darkness' was begun in mid-December 1898 and

finished within about a month – unusually rapid progress for Conrad, and evidence that the subject had taken possession of his mind and imagination. But by this time, of course, he had already been carrying those vivid and harrowing memories around with him for nearly a decade, just as he still retained in his bloodstream the malaria he had contracted in the Congo. In *A Personal Record* he was to describe his earlier story 'An Outpost of Progress' as 'the lightest part of the loot I carried off from Central Africa' and to add, 'the main portion being, of course, the *Heart of Darkness*'. In a sense, his involvement with Africa had begun even earlier, in his boyhood: elsewhere in *A Personal Record* he recalls that

> It was in 1868, when nine years old or thereabouts, that while looking at a map of Africa of the time and putting my finger on the blank space then representing the unsolved mystery of that continent, I said to myself with absolute assurance and an amazing audacity which are no longer in my character now: 'When I grow up I shall go *there*.'

He adds that *'there'* was 'the region of Stanley Falls, which in '68 was the blankest of blank spaces on the earth's figured surface'.

The scramble for Africa on the part of the European powers in the late nineteenth century led Leopold II of Belgium to summon a conference in Brussels in 1876 to discuss how (in that monarch's words) 'to open to civilisation the only part of our globe where Christianity has not penetrated and to pierce the darkness which envelops the entire population' (already one notes the key-word 'darkness', later to be deployed with such irony and ambiguity by Conrad). Leopold formed the International Association of the Congo, and eight years later another conference, held in Berlin, agreed that the Congo should become his personal property, which it remained for nearly a quarter of a century. There was during this time much exploitation of the natives and much tyranny and brutality – and also many fine-sounding protestations from the lips of the oppressors. In the year in which Conrad began his story, for instance, Leopold spoke of the mission of his agents (he never visited the Congo himself) as being 'to continue the development of civilisation in the centre of Equatorial Africa, receiving their inspiration directly from Berlin and Brussels'. He added, somewhat ominously, that these agents, 'placed face to face with primitive barbarism, grappling with sanguinary customs that date back thousands of years, . . . are obliged to reduce these gradually'. Such statements, with their plausible antithesis of 'civilisation' and 'barbarism', serve as a gloss on Conrad's tale and help to explain and justify his bitter irony.

That this historical and contemporary background was very much in Conrad's mind is indicated by a letter written to his publisher William Blackwood while he was still at work on the story (31 December 1898), in which he remarks that, despite the projected title, 'the narrative is not gloomy. The criminality of inefficiency and pure selfishness when tackling the civilizing work in Africa is a justifiable idea. The subject is of our time distinctly – though not topically treated'. In the event, he wrote a story that was not merely 'of our time' but which explores the human potentiality for corruption and evil – metaphysical brooding as well as topical satire – and this is perhaps what Conrad had in mind when he wrote to his friend Cunninghame Graham just over a month later that 'There are two more instalments in which the idea is so wrapped up in secondary notions that You – even You! may miss it. And also you must remember that I don't start with an abstract notion. I start with definite images and as their rendering is true some little effect is produced'. Those 'definite images' make 'Heart of Darkness' a closely and intricately woven work of poetic symbolism, which, published a generation before *The Waste Land*, needs to be read like a modernist poem rather than a sample of Victorian fiction.

The narrative method is that of 'Youth' with a considerable increase in complexity and significance. The establishing of the 'frame' situation takes longer, and the setting (the river Thames) has a relationship to that of the main action (the Congo). Moreover, the transition to the story-with-a-story, Marlow's reminiscences of his African experiences, is effected through a series of stages. The civilized after-dinner atmosphere, as in 'Youth' (from which the phrase 'bond of the sea' now reappears), leads to a reminder that from the Thames it is possible to travel 'to the uttermost ends of the earth'; then comes Marlow's abrupt reminder that ' "this also . . . has been one of the dark places of the earth" ', and his reference to the arrival in Britain of Roman colonists and exploiters (' "nineteen hundred years ago – the other day" '), and the parallel with Belgian exploitation of the Congo in the late nineteenth century is already beginning to take shape.

The density and many-layered significance of this short text have made it a favourite object of pedagogical and exegetical attention, and discussions of it in recent years have been very numerous. Some of the more profitable ones are collected in the Casebook edited by C. B. Cox (1981), and in the Norton Critical Edition of 'Heart of Darkness' edited by Robert Kimbrough (1963). Interpretations are legion, including those that see the story as a criticism of Christianity, a Freudian allegory, a version of the Grail quest, and an echo-chamber of Dante, Virgil, and the Buddhist scriptures. Two particularly full and helpful discussions will be found in Norman Sherry's *Conrad's Western World* (1971) and Ian Watt's *Conrad and the Nineteenth Century* (1980). Persuasively, Watt sees the story as predicting the impending collapse of Western civilization; but whatever interpretation may seem to the reader most compelling (and there is no obligation, of course, to opt for one at the expense of the rest), there can be no doubt that the experiences it records were crucial for Conrad. His biographer Jean-Aubry went so far as to say that 'Africa killed Conrad the sailor and strengthened Conrad the novelist', since the enforced idleness that illness contracted in the Congo forced upon him made him brood over his experiences and begin the process of transforming the raw material of life into art. Certainly, to this date, he had written nothing so fine apart from *The Nigger of the 'Narcissus'*.

'The End of the Tether' was begun in the spring of 1902, just after Conrad and Hueffer had completed their collaboration on *Romance*; and Hueffer claimed later, perhaps not without justification, that he had helped Conrad with the story. When the second of the six instalments intended for *Blackwood's Magazine* was nearly complete, the manuscript was accidentally destroyed – a serious matter, since publication was due to begin very shortly (Conrad had evidently cut things rather fine, as the accident was on 23 June and he wrote the next day that 'the MS. was due to-day in Edinburgh'). As a result, the story was written under considerable pressure in order to meet the deadlines: on 17 October Conrad told Garnett that he had been up for three nights trying to finish the story ('It was a matter of life and death').

Captain Whalley, the protagonist, has much in common with

Michael Henchard in Hardy's *The Mayor of Casterbridge*. An older man with a daughter whom he loves dearly, he comes to grief partly through ill-luck (he loses his savings through a bank failure, and he begins to lose his sight) but also through yielding to temptation after an upright life (he becomes involved in some shady business dealings). The ensuing moral discovery – that 'All his spotless life had fallen into the abyss' – leads to his death. Unlike the other two stories in the volume, 'The End of the Tether' uses the conventional third-person mode of narration. Perhaps for this reason an anonymous reviewer in the *Times Literary Supplement* (12 December 1902) thought it the best of the three ('much less clever, much less precious') – a view shared by Henry James, though not by later critics. Garnett found it a less remarkable piece of work than either 'Youth' or 'Heart of Darkness', but praised Conrad's depiction of Captain Whalley as 'the best piece of character painting he has yet achieved'.

TYPHOON AND OTHER STORIES

Three of the four stories in this collection are among Conrad's best, and the volume justifies the comment of a reviewer in the *Manchester Guardian* (23 April 1903) that 'Mr Conrad is now writing in the fulness of his power'. It was published by Heinemann on 22 April 1903, three of the stories having appeared previously in magazines, and received a very favourable reception – Sherry, indeed, describes it as 'overwhelming' and comments that 'one has the feeling that Conrad was on the verge of being overestimated'. The *Times Literary Supplement* (24 April 1903) reversed the kind of comparison between Conrad and Kipling, to Conrad's disadvantage, that had become commonplace, and declared that 'not even Kipling . . . has quite the same power of intense vividness'. The *Morning Post* (22 April 1903) said that, as a writer of short stories, 'Mr Kipling is the only one who can be compared with him . . . if we allow Mr Kipling to be supreme on land, Mr Conrad has no equal on the seas.'

'Typhoon' was published in the *Pall Mall Magazine* in three instalments (January–March 1902; illustrated by Maurice Greiffenhagen). It appears to have been written between September 1900 and January 1901. In 1919 Conrad added an 'Author's Note' in which he states that the central incident is based on real life but not on personal experience: he had heard it 'talked about in the East' but had 'never met anybody personally concerned in this affair'. The name of MacWhirr is borrowed from the captain under whom Conrad had served on the *Highland Forest*: see under 1887 in 'A Conrad Chronology' earlier in this volume. The 'Author's Note' also makes the important point that the real subject of the story is 'not the bad weather but the extraordinary complication brought into the ship's life at a moment of exceptional stress by the human element below her deck' (i.e. the coolies).

Superficially, the story offers a powerful account of appalling weather conditions at sea, and on this level it works extremely well: the description of the force of the typhoon and its effect on the

146

Nan-Shan is one of Conrad's finest pieces of descriptive writing. A notable feature of the narrative is his refusal to try to improve on, or even to repeat, his own achievement: the second phase of the typhoon occurs in the space between the fifth and sixth chapters and goes entirely undescribed.

Beyond this, the story is a study of Captain MacWhirr, 'irresponsive' and 'unruffled', 'having just enough imagination to carry him through each successive day' and 'faithful to facts, which alone his consciousness reflected'. 'Facts' and 'imagination' are to turn out to be contrasting key-words of the story, and the dramatic and psychological heart of it is exposed in the final paragraph of the first chapter: a man who

> had sailed over the surface of the oceans as some men go skimming over the years of existence to sink gently into a placid grave, ignorant of life to the last, without ever having been made to see all it may contain of perfidy, of violence, and of terror

is exposed to the 'immeasurable strength' and the 'immoderate wrath' of 'the passionate sea'. At this point, and again later, we perceive that the simple narrative can also be read as a parable.

Confronted with what he calls 'dirty weather', MacWhirr's practical philosophy is not to try to evade it but to meet it head-on: as he tells Jukes, ' "A gale is a gale, . . . and a full-powered steamship has got to face it. There's just so much dirty weather knocking about the world, and the proper thing is to go through it . . ." '. At this point in the story his lack of imagination is a positive virtue. But even he is affected, and even his unpractised imagination is stirred, towards the end of chapter 5, when he puts a box of matches carefully back in its place and it occurs to him that 'perhaps he would never have occasion to use that box any more': the match-box becomes 'the symbol of all these little habits that chain us to the weary round of life'. He has been seriously discomposed, and has felt a sense of 'dismay' reaching 'the very seat of his composure', by finding that the typhoon has intruded on his well-ordered arrangements – 'all the things that had their safe appointed places' have been thrown around as if by some vandal. But a few lines later he reaches out for a towel and finds that that at least is in its appointed place. As Guerard aptly says, 'This humble moment is the story's climax', and MacWhirr's next remark shows a return of dogged determination: ' "She may come out of it yet." '

The final chapter of this masterly tale shows that this crisis in MacWhirr's life has been completely misunderstood by those who know him best: his wife, reading a letter in which he tells her about the typhoon, totally fails to perceive the drama of his self-revelation; and the last words are the uncomprehending verdict of Jukes – ' "I think that he got out of it very well for such a stupid man." '

'Amy Foster' was serialized in the weekly *Illustrated London News* from 14 to 28 December 1901 (illustrations by Gunning King); Conrad may have appreciated the irony by which this story of a community's lack of charity appeared over the Christmas period. It was written quite quickly in May–June 1901, immediately after 'Falk'. The germ of the story seems to have been suggested by Hueffer, and it is not difficult to see that the simple but powerful situation of a shipwrecked man's failure to communicate with the ignorant folk among whom he found himself would make a strong personal appeal to Conrad. Personal tragedy, exile, linguistic isolation, and almost intolerable loneliness all conspire to make the protagonist's plight intensely pathetic.

A Central European peasant, lured by false promises, decides to seek his fortune in America but is cast away and washed ashore near an English village. The villagers treat him brutally, regarding him as a drunken tramp or a madman; the only person who makes a gesture of kindness is the slow-witted servant Amy Foster, whom he at length marries. She is bewildered by his wish to teach their child his native language; and when he falls ill and in his delirium babbles in a strange tongue she abandons him and he dies alone. (Conrad himself was to revert to Polish in his final illness.)

The story is narrated by a country doctor, and the protagonist's desolating loneliness – largely arising from his failure to understand or be understood in English – is movingly rendered. As the doctor says, 'He could talk to no one, and had no hope of ever understanding anybody'; and again, 'It is indeed hard upon a man to find himself a lost stranger, helpless, incomprehensible, and of a mysterious origin, in some obscure corner of the earth'.

'To-morrow', published in the *Pall Mall Magazine* in August 1902 (illustrated by Gunning King), is the only story in the collection that falls short of being a masterpiece. (Arthur

Quiller-Couch rather surprisingly thought it the best.) It is also
the shortest of the four tales. It seems to have been written at the
end of 1901 or the very beginning of 1902, and was sent to
Conrad's agent, Pinker, on 16 January 1902 with the comment
that it was ' "Conrad" adapted down to the needs of a magazine'.
A couple of years later Conrad turned it into a one-act play and it
was staged under the title *One Day More*; the dramatic version was
published in 1919.

Captain Hagberd is an elderly widower of eccentric habits and
on retiring from the sea has settled in the little seaport of
Colebrook. His only son has long ago run away to sea, and the old
man becomes obsessed with preparations for the return that he
believes to be imminent. He plans that the returned prodigal shall
marry the young woman who lives next door with her tyrannical
blind father; but when the son, responding to a newspaper
advertisement, does return, he turns out to be a rolling stone who
has no intention of settling down. Moreover, his father fails to
recognize him and continues to insist monomaniacally that his
son will come 'tomorrow'. The girl, for whom the son's coming
has been the only faint hope of escape, is left in despair between
the fat, selfish blind man and the 'old man shouting of his trust in
an everlasting tomorrow' (the captain being afflicted, of course,
with another kind of blindness). On the final page of the story she
'begins to totter silently back towards her stuffy little inferno of a
cottage', which has earlier been referred to in Dantean terms
('Abandon hope all ye who enter here'). The story is thus an
attempt to present hell in terms not of medieval theology but of
commonplace modern lives.

'Falk' was written immediately after 'Typhoon' and finished in
May 1901. Conrad later commented that it was 'partly biographical being an episode in the story of my first command'. The
subject of cannibalism made it unpalatable to editors, and there
was no magazine publication.

Conrad begins with his favourite device of a masculine
dinner-gathering: 'in a small river-hostelry' on the Thames
estuary, the narrator of the frame-story hears a tale recounted by
one of the party, 'a man of over fifty, that had commanded ships
for a quarter of a century'. The episode has taken place 'many
years ago . . . in a certain Eastern seaport' when the story-teller
was 'not thirty yet', and concerns a German skipper, Hermann,
whose wife and children live with him on his ship and whose

existence is thoroughly bourgeois: '. . . he toiled upon the seas, in
his own way, much as a shopkeeper works behind his counter'.
The ship is named the *Diana* and is 'a most innocent old ship, and
seemed to know nothing of the wicked sea, as there are on shore
households that know nothing of the corrupt world'; later it is
described as 'devoted to the support of domestic virtues like any
grocer's shop on shore'. As this summary indicates, the situation
bears some resemblance to that of Captain MacWhirr in
'Typhoon' – by an ironic paradox, the seasoned sailor has
somehow remained untouched by the elemental violence of the
natural world; but the tone in 'Falk' is more humorous (the
story-teller describes it as 'an absurd episode'). There is humorous irony, for instance, in the naming of the ship, which is a family
home, after Diana, the goddess of chastity. The theme of the story
is the confrontation of childlike innocence (a key-word) with the
knowledge of the extremes of suffering, violence and horror.

The family group includes the nubile niece of Hermann – a
goddess-like creature of magnificent proportions. Falk, the Scandinavian owner of a tug-boat, becomes infatuated with her,
frequents Hermann's family circle, and wishes to marry her. But if
Hermann represents 'venerable innocence' and unawareness of
the harsh realities of existence, Falk represents the 'elemental'
and the semi-human (he is compared at one point to a centaur).
Falk also has something of the Ancient Mariner in him: he
confesses that being alone is becoming intolerable to him, and at
last is impelled to tell of a past experience that haunts him and
that he can no longer keep to himself. On a disastrous voyage in
southern latitudes, the crew have been reduced to starvation and
Falk alone has survived by cunning, ruthless will, murder and
cannibalism. Hermann is appalled by this revelation of the
unsuspected possibilities of life; but he quickly comes to terms
with the situation and convinces himself that it has probably been
exaggerated – in other words, he chooses to preserve his moral
blindness – and Falk marries the girl.

'Falk' is a masterly narrative in Conrad's most accomplished
ironic vein and has (unusually for Conrad) a very agreeably
astringent humour. The horrific truth about Falk's past is
revealed only towards the end of the story; but numerous clues
have been planted – he lives on rice and fish, for instance, and flies
into a rage if his crew attempt to cook meat. More subtly, Conrad
uses gastronomic imagery: 'Hermann's excitement suddenly

went off the boil as when you remove a saucepan from the fire'. The earliest hint of the cannibalistic motif occurs in the second paragraph, where the dinner at the riverside inn is described as 'execrable' and the chops are singled out for condemnation:

> They brought forcibly to one's mind the night of ages when the primeval man, evolving the first rudiments of cookery from his dim consciousness, scorched lumps of flesh at a fire of sticks in the company of other good fellows; then, gorged and happy, sat him back among the gnawed bones to tell his artless tales of experience – the tales of hunger and hunt – and of women, perhaps!

With hindsight, one sees that the essence of the tale is contained in this sentence. The whole paragraph indeed is retrospectively, or on re-reading, rich in irony: compare 'He who hath known the bitterness of the Ocean shall have its taste for ever in his mouth'. The passage is echoed much later when the narrator of the story of Falk is offered chops at Schomberg's hotel.

Baines points out that, while tone and treatment are quite different, 'Falk' has something in common with 'Heart of Darkness'. Among contemporary reviewers, the *Morning Post* critic remarked somewhat quaintly that Conrad 'does not altogether shine as a humourist' (22 April 1903). An anonymous reviewer in the *Academy* (9 May 1903), however, was unusually perceptive both about this story and about Conrad's work as a whole:

> 'Falk' is a most remarkable study; it illustrates Mr Conrad's way in Mr Conrad's most elaborate manner. It is as certain that no other living author could have written it as that no other living author would have attempted it. In its way, the thing is architectural, or rather, like a mosaic, built up out of infinite fragments. The heart or secret of it is almost unimportant; we should have been content to let Falk's misfortune remain undiscovered. We are almost inclined to resent anything in the nature of a plot in Mr Conrad's work; he has no need of adventitious aids. He is an interpreter not of incidents mechanically contrived, but of moods and the human spirit.

It was not often that Edwardian critics saw that subject-matter and plot are much less important in Conrad than moral analysis and moral discovery, or that his allusive, suggestive, 'architectural' or mosaic-like technique demands that he be read in quite a different way from, say, Sir Walter Scott or Captain Marryat. Frederick Karl's verdict on the story (in *Joseph Conrad: the Three Lives*, pp. 512–13) seems to me quite unacceptable:

> Full of portentous trappings, 'Falk' finally comes across as a tale of survival in a primitive setting . . . left-handed work, a comic interlude, in which the taboo of eating man's flesh never achieves the intensity [Conrad] is striving for.

This is surely to mistake the tale's centre of gravity. Falk's narrative of his ordeal is rapid and condensed, and is placed near the end of the tale, in which it occupies only a small part. The theme is not 'survival' or cannibalism but innocence and experience, especially an innocence so armour-plated that the truth cannot penetrate it; and the tone, so far from being 'portentous', is engagingly light and ironic.

There is an interesting recent discussion of 'Falk' in Tony Tanner's essay ' "Gnawed Bones" and "Artless Tales" – Eating and Narrative in Conrad', in *Joseph Conrad: A Commemoration*, ed. Norman Sherry (1976).

A SET OF SIX

Each of the six stories in this volume carries a categorizing subtitle, and all had been previously published in magazines in 1906 or 1908. The book was published by Methuen of London in 1908 in an edition of 1500 copies; the American edition did not appear until 1915. *Critical Heritage* reprints an interesting selection of reviews together with Conrad's deeply-felt responses to them. W. L. Courtney (*Daily Telegraph*, 12 August 1908) declared that 'two, or, perhaps, three of the stories are masterpieces, while all of them stand at an exceedingly high level of workmanship and literary value'. In a review in the *Bookman* (October 1908), Edward Thomas described Conrad as 'a lord of language'. Edward Garnett reviewed the book in the *Nation* (22 August 1908) and seized the opportunity to answer some of the earlier reviewers. Conrad himself wrote to his publisher on 26 January 1908 that 'they are not studies – they touch no problem. They are just stories in which I've tried my best to be *simply entertaining*'.

'Gaspar Ruiz: A Romantic Tale' was serialized in the *Pall Mall Magazine* from July to October 1906 (illustrated by Cyrus Cuneo). It is set in Chile and seems to have been begun late in 1904, shortly after the completion of Conrad's South American novel, *Nostromo*, and finished in October 1905. The hero is a giant of a man who escapes a firing-squad, becomes a fugitive, and leads a band of rebels; in a siege he offers his body as a gun-carriage, but his back is broken. Beginning as a third-person narrative, it quickly turns into the reminiscences of an old man recalling his youth. Robert Lynd (*Daily News*, 10 August 1908) thought it 'worth all the rest of the book' and said that Conrad had written 'a story to compare with [Turgenev's] "A Lear of the Steppes" ' – a judgment that excited Conrad's scorn, who wrote to Garnett (21 August 1908) of the reviewer's 'incredible folly' in comparing 'that infernal magazine fake with the *Lear of the Steppes*!!!!' W. L. Courtney called it 'a little masterpiece'. In 1920 Conrad collaborated with Pinker on a film script based on this story and titled *Gaspar the Strong Man*; it was never produced and has not survived.

'The Informer: An Ironic Tale' appeared in *Harper's Magazine* in December 1906 (illustrated by Wolcott Hitchcock). It reads like an offshoot of *The Secret Agent*, a version of which had been completed and serialized by December 1906: the story deals with anarchists in London, the character of the Professor is briefly sketched, and the comment that 'anarchists, I suppose, have no families' hints ironically at Mr Verloc. A first-person frame-narrative contains the narrative of a 'Mr X'. Edward Garnett regarded it as the 'least successful' of the stories in the volume. It had been written in five days at the end of December 1905.

'The Brute: an Indignant Tale' concerns a ship that has the reputation of causing men's deaths and finally runs aground because the officer of the watch is occupied with a woman. (There is an intentional ambiguity at the opening, where 'she' appears to refer to a woman but actually designates the ship.) Again, a first-person frame-narrative accommodates the narrative of another speaker. Original publication was in the *Daily Chronicle* on 5 December 1906. Baines calls it 'little more than a pot-boiler'.

'An Anarchist: A Desperate Tale' was completed in December 1905 and appeared in *Harper's Magazine* in August 1906 (illustrated by Thornton Oakley). Set on a South American cattle estate, it shows that 'a little thing may bring about the undoing of a man'. The first-person narrator, a lepidopterist, tells how a decent French workman has been caught in the toils of anarchists and is now virtually the slave of a great capitalist enterprise.

'The Duel: A Military Tale' was serialized in the *Pall Mall Magazine* from January to May 1908 (illustrated by the well-known artist W. Russell Flint). The longest of the stories in this volume, it is set at the time of the Napoleonic Wars. Its third-person narrative relates how a quarrel begins over a triviality (an imaginary insult) and continues through many years against a background of war and politics. According to the 'Author's Note', the situation 'springs from a ten-line paragraph in a small provincial paper published in the South of France'. Conrad said that he had tried to catch 'the Spirit of the Epoch'; moral comment on the situation is provided by an old chevalier, who, on learning of the duel that has persisted for sixteen years, exclaims, ' "What manners! What horrible perversion of manliness!" '. W. L. Courtney (see above) opined that the story 'becomes tedious through its unnecessary length'; Garnett, on the other hand, praised it as 'a masterpiece of style' and 'in the unerring delicacy of its artistic strokes, . . . worthy of Turgenev'.

'Il Conde: A Pathetic Tale' was published in *Cassell's Magazine* in August 1908 (illustrated by Cyrus Cuneo). An old gentleman of hypersensitive nature is robbed and threatened in Naples, with devastating effect upon his personality. The first-person narrative incorporates the victim's own account of the incident.

'TWIXT LAND AND SEA

The volume contains three stories, all previously published, and appeared in London and New York in 1912 (the English publisher, Dent, printed 3500 copies). The critical reception was in general very favourable: the *Times Literary Supplement*, for instance, proclaimed the three stories 'each a masterpiece', and the *Observer* said that they were 'as good as anything Conrad has ever written, tales as good as any man might hope to write' (20 October 1912). As Norman Sherry points out, Conrad's return to the East for his settings was welcomed: as the *Spectator* put it (16 November 1912), 'He has returned with fresh vigour to his earlier course'.

'A Smile of Fortune' first appeared in the *London Magazine* in February 1911. Subtitled 'Harbour Story', it is the least satisfactory of the three stories collected in this volume. The narrator is the captain of a ship that visits a tropical island referred to as the 'Pearl of the Ocean' in order to collect a cargo of sugar. There he meets a ship's chandler, Jacobus, visits the latter's home, and is powerfully attracted to his daughter Alice – a wild, surly girl who is the illegitimate offspring of Jacobus's infatuation with a circus artiste. The girl is described in strongly physical, even erotic terms, and there appears to be a suggestion of symbolism in her setting, a beautiful garden in which she passes her days almost as a recluse or a prisoner. The captain falls in love with her, but after delays in getting the cargo aboard the time comes for him to leave the island, and he does so without committing himself to her. To ease his conscience he spends every penny he possesses on buying a load of potatoes from her father as an investment – an act that at first seems ludicrous but that turns out to be 'a smile of fortune' when he arrives in a colony where the potato harvest has failed and he is able to dispose of the potatoes at a handsome profit. Like 'The Secret Sharer' in the same volume, the story concerns a young captain's initiation through experience into a knowledge of the world; however, it lacks the intensity of the slightly earlier

156

story ('The Secret Sharer' was written towards the end of 1909, 'A Smile of Fortune' about a year later). Moreover, the obscure hints that the long-haired girl is a kind of Eve in a kind of Eden are no match for the rich and sustained symbolic power of 'The Secret Sharer'. The third story in the volume, 'Freya of the Seven Isles', presents a heroine who has something in common with the Alice of this story.

In his recent book *Conrad: the Later Fiction* (1982), Daniel R. Schwarz has suggested that the three stories share a common element:

> All three tales explore a young captain under stress. . . . The sea is no longer the simplified world of 'Typhoon' or 'The End of the Tether', where moral distinctions are clear. In these 1909–11 tales, a young captain is faced with circumstances and emotional traumas for which neither the maritime code nor his experience has prepared him.

According to Baines, certain elements in 'A Smile of Fortune' were 'drawn from Conrad's visit to Mauritius with his first command, the *Otago*'. Similar memories of his first command are at work in 'The Secret Sharer', which also makes use of an actual incident that occurred on the *Cutty Sark* in 1880, when the mate killed a seaman who disobeyed an order and was subsequently helped to escape by the captain. Conrad seems to have written the story very rapidly, and it achieves a remarkable momentum. It was published in *Harper's Magazine* in August and September 1910 (illustrated by W. J. Aylward).

The first person narrator of 'The Secret Sharer' is also the protagonist. The time and circumstances of his narration are not disclosed; but at one point he refers to 'this distance of years', so that the young captain is evidently recalling in middle age his own experiences at a crucial stage of his life, rather as Conrad was looking back on his youth in this and much of his fiction. The story opens with a ship 'anchored at the head of the Gulf of Siam' and its captain 'appointed to the command only a fortnight before'. We learn that it is his first command, that it has come upon him quite unexpectedly, and that he feels 'a stranger on board'. He also feels a good deal of anxiety and self-doubt as to whether he will prove equal to whatever trials the voyage may submit him to: 'I wondered how far I should turn out faithful to that ideal conception of one's own personality every man sets up for himself secretly' (a theme Conrad had already explored in *Lord Jim*). He reflects, with characteristic Conradian irony, that 'the sea was not likely to keep any special surprises expressly for my discomfiture'.

But out of the sea comes another young man, a fugitive from the *Sephora*, where he has (as he promptly announces) ' "killed a man" '. He is harboured by the captain, dressed in his clothes, and concealed in his cabin, none of the crew knowing of his presence, until, in an exciting conclusion, the captain takes the ship sufficiently (and perilously) near to the land to permit him to swim to safety. Throughout the story the escapee is frequently (indeed, over-insistently) referred to as the 'double' or 'other self' of the captain – earlier titles were 'The Second Self', 'The Secret Self', 'The Other Self' – and the reader naturally wonders whether he has any objective existence or is merely a hallucination of the other's overwrought brain. Conrad has taken care to plant evidence to enable this theory to be dismissed; but there is undoubtedly something spectral about Leggatt (his name perhaps suggests 'legate' in the sense of 'messenger' or 'deputy'), whose first appearance is ghost-like ('A headless corpse!' says the captain, whose own head is bent over the side of the ship).

The moral situation is fraught with paradoxes: Leggatt has saved the *Sephora* by killing a man; the captain, whose plain duty it is to hand him over to the proper authorities, shelters him and permits his escape. The outcome is that the captain finds himself: with the departure of Leggatt, his 'other self', who will be 'hidden forever from all friendly faces, to be a fugitive and a vagabond on the earth', he himself feels a sense of mature self-possession, 'the perfect communion of a seaman with his first command'.

The story is one of Conrad's best and has provoked extensive commentary. Albert Guerard's psychoanalytical interpretation sees Leggatt as a 'lower self' of the captain: he emerges from the deep (symbolizing the unconscious) and is 'the embodiment of a more instinctive, more primitive, less rational self'. This is a challenging reading of the story, but it raises certain difficulties; and Guerard's commentary may instructively be read in conjunction with Baines' dismissal of this approach. Among many other accounts, there is an interesting essay by F. R. Leavis in his *'Anna Karenina' and Other Essays* (1967). Leavis sees the theme of the story as 'the inescapable need for individual moral judgment, and for moral conviction that is strong and courageous enough to forget codes and to defy law and codified morality and justice'.

'Freya of the Seven Isles' appeared in the *Metropolitan Magazine* in April 1912 (illustrated by Clifford W. Ashley) and in the *London Magazine* in July 1912 (illustrated by Gilbert Holiday). It had been completed in February 1911, and on the fifteenth of that month Conrad had described it in a letter to Warrington Dawson as 'quite good magazine stuff, quite Conradesque (in the easier style)'. After the appearance of *'Twixt Land and Sea* he wrote to Edward Garnett even more dismissively: 'I daresay *Freya* is pretty rotten. On the other hand the *Secret Sharer*, between you and me, is *it*. Eh? No damned tricks with girls there. Eh? Every word fits and there's not a single uncertain note' (5 November 1912). These comments do scant justice to 'Freya', which, though certainly inferior to 'The Secret Sharer', is narrated with considerable power and conviction. It is 'Conradesque' in setting (the East Indies) and theme (idealistic love destroyed by malevolent sexual jealousy), and 'in the easier style' in the sense that the narrative is straightforwardly chronological, even though the narrator has evidently acquired his knowledge of the events piecemeal.

Freya is a beautiful motherless girl who, like Alice in 'A Smile of Fortune', has very long hair; she lives on an island with her weak and unworldly father, a Dane called Nielsen (also known as Nelson). Jasper Allen, the owner of a trading brig, the *Bonito*, falls in love with her, and they plan to elope as soon as she reaches the age of twenty-one and to live happily ever after on the gleaming white boat that is fitted up like a gentleman's yacht and is Jasper's pride and joy. But a brutal Dutch naval lieutenant, Heemskirk, who commands a gunboat, becomes attracted to Freya and, possessed by jealousy of Jasper, contrives that the yacht is seized and run aground on a reef and the young man charged wrongfully with gun-running. Grieved by the loss of his boat, Jasper sinks into a kind of lethargy; and the girl falls ill and dies of pneumonia.

The moral contrast between the young couple and the Dutch-man is reinforced by symbolism that recalls *Lord Jim*:

> . . . the charmingly fresh and resolute Freya, the innocently round-eyed old Nelson, Jasper, keen, long limbed, lean faced, admirably self-contained, in his manner, because inconceiv-ably happy under the eyes of his Freya; all three tall, fair, and

blue-eyed in various shades, and amongst them the swarthy, arrogant, black-haired Dutchman, shorter nearly by a head, and so much thicker than any of them that he seemed to be a creature capable of inflating himself, a grotesque specimen of mankind from some other planet.

Like Alice in 'A Smile of Fortune', Freya is a kind of Eve-figure or mythological being (at one point she is addressed as ' "You Scandinavian Goddess of Love." '); and the life she hopes to live with Jasper has an idealized, otherworldly quality. Heemskirk, on the other hand, is of the earth earthy, being physically repulsive with his fatness, his bullet head, and his hooked nose, as well as surly and brutal, and strongly recalls the toad ('a creature capable of inflating itself') that is Satan's disguise in *Paradise Lost*. Five times he is compared to a beetle or a black beetle (compare the beetle/butterfly symbolism in *Lord Jim*), and he is associated with blackness as the younger man is associated with immaculate whiteness. Later in the story, for instance, when the two boats encounter each other on the high seas,

the smoke belching out suddenly from [the gunboat's] short black funnel rolled between the masts of the *Bonito*, obscuring for a moment the sunlit whiteness of her sails, consecrated to the service of love.

The sailing ship and the steam-driven gunboat are a metonymic expression of the contrasting natures of the men who command them; for Jasper, the *Bonito* (Spanish for 'beautiful') is inextricably blended with his love for Freya, and when the boat is lost to him – on the reef it is still visible, its whiteness slowly turning to a dirty grey – an essential ingredient in his dream of love fulfilled has been lost, and he abandons all hope of a happy outcome for his life and surrenders himself to a paralysing loss of will.

The volume, published in 1915 in an edition of 3500 copies, brings together four stories published between 1911 and 1914 and adds an interesting 'Author's Note'.

'The Planter of Malata' was written in November–December 1913 and originally titled 'The Assistant'. It appeared in a New York periodical, the *Metropolitan Magazine*, in June and July 1914 and was illustrated by Frederic Dorr Steele. Felicia Moorsom, the daughter of a famous scientist and philosopher, has been engaged to a man in England, but when he is accused of embezzlement she has believed in his guilt and he has left the country. Subsequently she receives proof that he is innocent, and, accompanied by her father and an aunt, sets out to seek him in order to set matters right by marrying him. Her search brings her at length to a 'great colonial city' in the Antipodes (presumably Sydney), where she meets Geoffrey Renouard, who is running a silk farm on a nearby island. He falls passionately in love with her, but eventually realizes that the man she is seeking is his own former assistant, who has recently died. In order to prevent her from going away, he tells her that the man is on the island but says nothing of his death. She goes to the island, where he takes her to the man's grave and tells her of his own love. She refuses him, and departs; and Renouard commits suicide by setting out 'to swim beyond the confines of life . . . – his eyes fixed on a star!'. His incurable romanticism makes him a blood-brother of such Conradian heroes as Lord Jim; ironically enough, the woman who rejects him is made of the same stuff, her unfulfilled mission being no more than a quixotic gesture. The story's central situation has power, but its infatuated hero does not entirely carry conviction. The manuscript is dated 14 December 1913. Baines points out that in its 'extreme romanticism' it has something in common with 'Freya of the Seven Isles' (see *'Twixt Land and Sea* above).

'The Partner' appeared in *Harper's Magazine* in November 1911 (illustrated by Anton Otto Fischer). It concerns the wrecking of a ship in order to obtain the insurance money, and is not unfairly dismissed by Baines as 'an obvious pot-boiler'.

'The Inn of the Two Witches' appeared in the *Pall Mall Magazine* in March 1913 and in the New York *Metropolitan Magazine* in May 1913 (illustrated by H. J. Mowat), having been written towards the end of 1912. Set in Spain during the Peninsular War, it tells how a British naval officer goes in search of a sailor who has been sent on a mission and has disappeared. In a lonely inn he discovers the sailor's body and narrowly escapes sharing his fate: he has been suffocated by a four-poster bed with a top that can be lowered by a mechanism operated in the next room, this crime having been regularly perpetrated by the avaricious and witch-like women who keep the inn. In his 'Author's Note' Conrad mentions that a reviewer had hinted that the idea was taken from 'a tale called *A very strange Bed* published in *Household Words* in 1852 or 54' (the story, actually called 'A Terribly Strange Bed', was by Wilkie Collins and had appeared in Dickens' magazine on 24 April 1852). Conrad disclaims all knowledge of the earlier story and states that the germ of his tale was taken from an historical source. Even if Collins' story were his basis, he certainly improves on it; and Baines dismissal of it as 'a story more suitable for boys than for adults' seems distinctly grudging. There is genuine horror in the scene in which the officer discovers the sailor's corpse, and his grief at the death of a brave and loyal comrade raises it above the level of the mere 'spooky tale'.

'Because of the Dollars' appeared until the title 'Lauching Anne' in the *Metropolitan Magazine* (New York) in September 1914 (illustrated by Frederic Dorr Steele), having been written at the end of 1913. Under its earlier title it was dramatized by Conrad in 1921. Set in the Malay Archipelago, it tells how Captain Davidson, who is carrying a cargo of dollars, is plotted against by a group of villains. They plan to murder him and steal the money, but he is warned by a wretched woman on whom he has taken pity and they are foiled. The woman is killed as an act of revenge by the ringleader of the plotters; Davidson, feeling acute remorse, adopts her son and is recompensed for his charitable deed by incurring the suspicion of his mean-spirited wife, who believes the child to be his own. Although superficially a tale of villainy outwitted, therefore, it ends on a serious and even pessimistic note. Davidson's name suggests that he may conceivably be seen as a Christ-figure, with the woman as a Magdalene.

TALES OF HEARSAY

Conrad's seventh and last collection of stories was published posthumously in 1925, with a preface by R. B. Cunninghame Graham, and brings together four stories, all published a number of years earlier in magazines: 'The Warrior's Soul' (*Land and Water*, 29 March 1917), 'Prince Roman' (*Oxford & Cambridge Review*, October 1911, and *Metropolitan Magazine*, January 1912), 'The Tale' (*Strand Magazine*, October 1917), and 'The Black Mate' (*London Magazine*, April 1908). Richard Curle gave the volume its title.

'The Warrior's Soul' was written in 1916 and, with 'The Tale', seems to have been Conrad's only production during that barren and anxious year. It is a wartime story but set a hundred years back, in the Napoleonic period which Conrad, like his contemporary Hardy, found so fascinating, and to which he was to turn again in his last novel, *The Rover*, a few years later, as well as in his unfinished novel *Suspense*. By this stage in his career Conrad was turning away from personal experience as a source of fictional material, and the source of the story was found in a book of French memoirs. Baines describes it as 'a dramatic story and far from negligible'.

'Prince Roman' was written somewhat earlier, towards the end of 1910, and at about the same time as 'A Smile of Fortune'. Its source is in Conrad's early years in Poland – partly on his meeting, during his childhood, with a certain Prince Roman Sanguszko, and partly on the memoirs of his Uncle Tadeusz published in 1900 – and it seems to have been originally intended to form part of an autobiographical work.

'The Tale', finished on 30 October 1916, is a story of the Great War and hence related, and complementary, to 'The Warrior's Soul'. It also bears, as Baines has pointed out, a significant relationship to Conrad's short novel *The Shadow-Line*, written in the previous year, the story being 'almost an exact antithesis' to the novel in its moral theme.

163

The last story in the volume, 'The Black Mate', is perhaps the most puzzling item in all Conrad's work. In 1886 Conrad seems to have submitted a story with this title for a competition in the popular British magazine *Tit-Bits*; his entry was unsuccessful, and the story seems to have been lost. If it ever existed – and it is very hard to imagine why Conrad should have invented the episode – then it was apparently his first attempt at authorship. Later he was vague about the matter, and he usually maintained that *Almayer's Folly* represented his first steps as a writer. In 1922 he wrote that 'My memories of this tale are confused. I have a notion that it was first written some time in the late eighties and retouched later'. But by this time the second 'Black Mate' – the one published in the *London Magazine* in 1908 – was already fourteen years old, and Conrad's memory was notoriously unreliable. What he can have meant by 'retouched' is unclear: it seems to imply the survival of the earlier manuscript, and yet nothing else suggests this. Jessie Conrad denied that there was any connection between the two stories; she insisted that she had given Conrad the idea for the 1908 story, and according to her version the two stories had only a title in common. The surviving story is a slight and light-hearted anecdote.

Collaborations

The suggestion for a collaboration between Conrad and Ford seems to have come from Conrad, though (as Najder points out) he may have been prompted by Edward Garnett. As it turned out, however, he played only a minor role in their three collaborations (*The Inheritors*, *Romance*, and *The Nature of a Crime*), and to regard these works as part of the corpus of Conrad's fiction is perhaps stretching the point a little.

Soon after their initial meeting in 1898, the two writers seem to have agreed to collaborate on an historical novel, *Seraphina* (renamed *Romance* at a much later stage) that Ford had already begun. Progress was slow – on 7 January 1902 Conrad wrote, '*Seraphina* seems to hang about me like a curse' – and in the event their first completed collaboration was *The Inheritors*. *Romance* was completed in March 1902, and their hope of scoring a decided commercial success was disappointed: their literary agent, Pinker, was unsuccessful in his attempts to place it as a serial, and even after it had been subjected to drastic cutting towards the end of the year no magazine editor would take it. It was published in volume form on 16 October 1903, and its critical reception was lukewarm.

Three weeks after publication, Conrad wrote: 'I consider *Romance* as something of no importance; I collaborated on it at a time when it was impossible for me to do anything else.' It is tempting to suggest that his attitude might have been very different if the novel had been a resounding success with the public; moreover, as Najder reminds us, it is simply untrue that Conrad worked on it when it was 'impossible' for him to 'do anything else', since its composition belongs to the period that produced 'Typhoon', 'Amy Foster', and other stories. Karl finds the book 'uneven' and lacking in coherence, and plausibly attributes this to the fact that Conrad and Ford each wrote portions of it but did not thoroughly revise the work as a whole.

Conrad had written to Galsworthy as soon as *Romance* was completed (10 March 1902): 'I do really hope it will hit the taste of the street', and it seems to have been an unblushing attempt to capitalize on the popularity of the kind of tale of adventure associated with Robert Louis Stevenson, H. Rider Haggard, and Anthony Hope. *The Inheritors*, in contrast, takes the scientific romances of H. G. Wells as its model: Najder describes it as 'a satirical fantasy à clef', and Conrad himself (who does not seem to have taken it very seriously, and whose part in its composition was in any case minimal) referred to it as 'a sort of skit'. Published on 26 June 1901, it was again a commercial failure. The grounds for taking it seriously as part of Conrad's achievement are even more slender than with *Romance*: Ford, indeed, claimed that Conrad had written no more than a thousand words or so, and for once he may be believed. Conrad wrote to him (12 November 1899): '. . . the *work* is all yours – I have shared only a little of your worry', and Najder glosses this observation as follows:

> Conrad's participation in *The Inheritors* consisted almost entirely of advising Ford, or rather inciting him to revise the manuscript, and of negotiating with publishers. Ford was responsible for both the idea and almost the entire text. Conrad's name helped sell the book.

As with *Romance*, Conrad joined in a rescue-attempt on a manuscript that Ford already had under way: he had been working on the novel for several months when, in early October 1899, he showed the opening chapters to Conrad. The latter's criticism and encouragement continued throughout the winter months, and the book was finished by 16 March 1900.

Karl has characterized the commercial aims of these collaborations as follows:

> The twin thrust of the collaborations was clear, to reach the audience in two popular areas: hit it high, with a sophisticated science-fiction tale full of political savvy; and hit it fairly low, in the region of pirates, adventure, and romance.

But neither achieved popularity or, for that matter, literary excellence. Their third and final collaboration was shorter and even slighter than these: the novella *The Nature of a Crime*, written in 1906 and published in the *English Review* under the pseudonym of Baron Ignatz von Aschendorf.

Non-Fictional Prose

THE MIRROR OF THE SEA

At the beginning of 1902 Conrad spoke of writing 'some autobiographical matter about Ships, skippers, and an adventure or two'; the result was *The Mirror of the Sea*, a collection of essays published in 1906, which according to Frederick R. Karl 'began as a somewhat loose collaboration with Ford, with the latter jogging Conrad's memory and taking notes as Conrad dictated'. Subtitled 'Memories and Impressions', the book consists of a series of reminiscences of, and meditations on, the sea, ships and sailors. The 'Author's Note' (added in 1919) describes it as 'a very intimate revelation' in which the author has 'attempted to lay bare with the unreserve of a last hour's confession the terms of my relation with the sea', and as a tribute to 'the ultimate shapers of my character, convictions, and, in a sense, destiny – to the imperishable sea, to the ships that are no more, and to the simple men who have had their day'.

The book is uneven in quality: some sections, such as that titled 'Initiation', are in Conrad's best vein, but others, such as 'Rulers of East and West', contain some embarrassing 'fine writing'. As the phrases quoted at the end of the previous paragraph suggest, a strain of nostalgic regret runs throughout: Conrad is preoccupied by the 'vanished generations' of sailing ships, 'blown off the face of the sea by a puff of steam'. Sailing, he makes it clear, was an art, not a matter of technology, and the seaman an artist, his life involving an 'intimacy with nature' and a 'single-handed struggle with something much greater than yourself'. The praise is sung of 'the honour of labour' and of those who, however humbly, do their 'little share of the world's work with proper efficiency' (for a parallel in the fiction one may turn to the closing lines of *The Nigger of the 'Narcissus'*). The book brings home to the reader very impressively how strong in Conrad's sensibility was the sense of loss – not only of country, family and language, but of his vocation as seaman and specifically of the vanished days of sailing-ships. This is presumably what Conrad had in mind in describing the book in a letter of 30 May 1906 as 'a record of a phase, now nearly vanished, of a certain kind of activity, sympathetic to the inhabitants of this Island' and, more generally, as 'an imaginative rendering of a reminiscent mood'. The epithet 'imaginative' in that last phrase warns us, perhaps, that this is, at least in places, fictionalized rather than 'straight' autobiography and not very different in kind from such stories as 'Youth' and 'Heart of Darkness' which draw heavily on personal experience without adhering consistently to it.

A PERSONAL RECORD

Under the title *Some Reminiscences* this appeared in the *English Review* from December 1908 to June 1909. It subsequently appeared in volume form under the same title (London, 1912) in an edition of 1000 copies; the title used for the American edition, *A Personal Record*, was from 1916 used for all editions, the original title becoming a subtitle. The original preface ('A Familiar Preface') states the purpose of the book as being 'to give the record of personal memories by presenting faithfully the feelings and sensations connected with the writing of my first book and with my first contact with the sea'. In Chapter 5 the parallel between the pains of authorship and those of seamanship is developed: writing for Conrad was

> a creative effort in which mind and will and conscience are engaged to the full, hour after hour, day after day, away from the world, and to the exclusion of all that makes life really lovable and gentle – something for which a material parallel can only be found in the everlasting sombre stress of the westward winter passage round Cape Horn.

The book contains much interesting autobiographical material, including recollections of Conrad's father, as well as important comments on 'the question of language' in the course of which he writes:

> The impression of my having exercised a choice between the two languages, French and English, both foreign to me, has got abroad somehow. That impression is erroneous. . . . The truth of the matter is that my faculty to write in English is as natural as any other aptitude with which I might have been born. I have a strange and overpowering feeling that it had always been an inherent part of myself. English was for me neither a matter of choice nor adoption. The merest idea of choice had never entered my head. And as to adoption – well, yes, there was adoption; but it was I who was adopted by the genius of the language. . . . If I had not written in English I would not have written at all.

The story that Conrad had made a conscious choice between French and English before embarking on a career of authorship seems to have been promulgated by Sir Hugh Clifford, and was repeated by Hugh Walpole in his 1916 book on Conrad, giving Conrad the occasion to insist (in a letter of 7 June 1918) that the notion was 'absurd', to say that 'When I wrote the first words of *Almayer's Folly*, I had been already for years and years *thinking* in English', and to repeat the substance of the last sentence in the above quotation from *A Personal Record* ('You may take it from me that if I had not known English I wouldn't have written a line for print, in my life'). Earlier he had been upset by a remark by the reviewer Robert Lynd, who had described him in the *Daily News* (10 August 1908) as 'a Pole, who writes English by choice, as it were, rather than by nature'. The grievance was a recurring (and an entirely reasonable) one with Conrad, who even earlier had remarked in a letter to Garnett (October 1907) that he had been 'so cried up of late as a sort of freak, an amazing bloody foreigner writing in English'.

The significant word 'choice' occurs in *A Personal Record* again in a different context, when Conrad recalls his early resolution that 'if I was to be a seaman then I would be a British seaman and no other. It was a matter of deliberate choice'. Almost on the last page of the book he recalls the moment when he heard English spoken for the first time by natives and once again uses the same word:

... the speech of my secret choice, of my future, of long friendships, of the deepest affections, of hours of toil and hours of ease, and of solitary hours too, of books read, of thoughts pursued, of remembered emotions – of my very dreams!

It may not be going too far to suggest that, in reiterating his 'choice' in this way, Conrad was throwing the word back in the teeth of the hapless Lynd.

The book also contains some meditations on art such as the following from the end of the opening chapter:

Imagination, not invention, is the supreme master of art as of life. An imaginative and exact rendering of authentic memories may serve worthily that spirit of piety towards all things human which sanctions the conceptions of a writer of tales, and the emotions of the man reviewing his own experience.

Conrad wrote no autobiography in the strict sense of the word, but *A Personal Record* and *The Mirror of the Sea*, together with his splendid and important letters, find their origin in the mind of a 'man reviewing his own experience'.

NOTES ON LIFE AND LETTERS

Published in 1921, this volume collects essays published in various periodicals and, with the posthumous *Last Essays* (see below), brings together the bulk of Conrad's writing in this form. The 'Author's Note' anticipates the charge that the assembled pieces are no more than trifles by asserting that 'All these things had a place in my life'. He warns the reader that he will not find 'Conrad *en pantoufles*' ('in slippers', i.e., in relaxed or informal mood), though the volume is 'as near as I shall ever come to *deshabille* in public'. The 'Note' also states that the essays had originally appeared between 1898 and 1920, that only 'Note on the Polish Problem' was previously unpublished, and that the collection had 'more to do with life than with letters' (there are in fact thirteen items in each section, but it is true that those on 'Life' are on average considerably longer). The section on 'Life' includes the interesting autobiographical piece 'Poland Revisited' (1915) and several other pieces on political topics. That on

'Letters' includes essays on James, Daudet, Maupassant, Anatole France, Turgenev and Crane.

LAST ESSAYS

Richard Curle's introduction to this volume, published in 1926, states that the book contains 'the last essays of Joseph Conrad': most of the items originally appeared after the publication of *Notes on Life and Letters*, and the two books together 'may be said to contain practically all Conrad's miscellaneous writings'. Among the twenty items are essays on Crane and Galsworthy (the latter was written earlier but seems to have been omitted from the 1920 volume by an oversight), a short preface to Jessie Conrad's *A Handbook of Cookery for a Small House*, and the 1890 'Congo Diary', important in connection with *Heart of Darkness*.

Plays

Motivated by the high financial rewards available to the author of a long-running play, Conrad often dallied with the idea of writing for the theatre and at various times planned a number of adaptations of his fiction, alone or in collaboration, not all of which came to fruition. His one-act play *One Day More*, adapted from his short story 'To-morrow', was produced in London in 1905; according to one of Conrad's letters. George Bernard Shaw, who was enjoying a considerable success as a dramatist at that time, was 'enthusiastic' (the same letter adds modestly, but not too modestly, 'I don't think I am a dramatist'). A limited edition appeared in 1919 and another edition (New York) in 1920. Another short story, 'Because of the Dollars', was dramatized by Conrad in 1921 under the title *Laughing Anne*; this play in two acts seems never to have been produced on the stage, though it was printed in 1923 and also filmed. Also in 1921 Conrad had privately printed a dramatization in four acts of his novel *The Secret Agent*, and a different version in three acts was produced in London in November of the following year. It ran for only a few performances, but Conrad claimed to be 'affected . . . not at all' by the unfavourable reviews it received: 'I was amused by their touching unanimity in damning the play. It was like a chorus of parrots'. According to Ian Watt, 'The play followed the novel closely, and used much of the dialogue. The necessities of staging, however, meant that the action had to be concentrated in a few places' (for further details, see Watt's volume on *The Secret Agent* in the Casebook Series [1973], p. 83). Conrad refers wryly to this enterprise in his 'Author's Note' to the novel: 'lately, circumstances . . . have compelled me to strip this tale of the literary robe of indignant scorn it has cost me so much to fit on it decently, years

173

ago [that is, the prevailing ironic tone of the novel]. I have been forced, so to speak, to look upon its bare bones. I confess that it makes a grisly skeleton' – a fitting epitaph, perhaps, on Conrad's brief adventures in the theatre. *Laughing Anne* and *One Day More* were published together in 1924, with an introduction by Galsworthy, and all three plays appeared in a single volume in 1934.

For Conrad's adaptation of his story 'Gaspar Ruiz', which has not survived, see the section 'Filmography' below.

Filmography

The following information is provided in respect of film versions of the various works by Conrad: (1) title of film; (2) date of release; (3) country of production; (4) production company/distributing organisation; (5) director. All are English-language films unless otherwise stated.

'Because of the Dollars' (*Within the Tides*)
(1) *Laughing Anne*; (2) 1954; (3) UK; (4) Republic Pictures/Imperadio; (5) Herbert Wilcox.
'The Duel' (*A Set of Six*)
(1) *The Duellists*; (2) 1977; (3) USA; (4) Cinema International Corp.
'Gaspar Ruiz' (*A Set of Six*)
Conrad wrote a screenplay based on this story in 1920 and titled it *The Strong Man*. It was never produced or published.
'Heart of Darkness' (*Typhoon*)
Francis Ford Coppola's *Apocalypse Now* (1979, USA) is loosely based on Conrad's story.
Lord Jim
(1) *Lord Jim*; (2) 1925; (3) USA; (4) Famous Players-Lasky/Paramount; (5) Victor Fleming.
(1) *Lord Jim*; (2) 1965; (3) USA; (4) Columbia Pictures/Keep Films; (5) Richard Brooks.
Nostromo
(1) *The Silver Treasure*; (2) 1926; (3) USA; (4) Fox Film Corporation; (5) Rowland V. Lee.
An Outcast of the Islands
(1) *An Outcast of the Islands*; (2) 1951; (3) UK; (4) London Films/British Lion; (5) Carol Reed.
The Rescue
(1) *The Rescue*; (2) 1929; (3) USA; (4) Goldwyn/United Artists; (5) Herbert Brenon.
Romance
(1) *The Road to Romance*; (2) 1927; (3) USA; (4) Metro-Goldwyn-Mayer; (5) John S. Robertson.

The Rover

(1) *L'Aventurier*; (2) 1966; (3) Italy; (5) Terence Young and Giancarlo Zagni. (Italian-language.)

The Secret Agent

(1) *Sabotage*; (2) 1936; (3) UK; (4) Gaumont British; (5) Alfred Hitchcock.

'The Secret Sharer' (*'Twixt Land and Sea*)

(1) *Face to Face*; (2) 1952; (3) USA; (4) Theasquare/RKO; (5) John Brahm and Bretaigne Windust.

(1) *The Secret Sharer*; (2) 1972; (3) USA; (4) Encyclopaedia Britannica Short Story Showcase. (This is a 30-minute dramatisation followed by an 11-minute discussion made for educational purposes.)

Under Western Eyes

(1) *Razumov*; (2) 1938; (3) France; (4) Productions André Daven/Brandon Films/Garrison Films; (5) Marc Allegret. (French-language.)

Victory

(1) *Victory*; (2) 1919; (3) USA; (4) Paramount–Artcraft; (5) Maurice Tourneur.

(1) *Victory*; (2) 1920; (3) UK.

(1) *Dangerous Paradise*; (2) 1930; (3) USA; (4) Famous Players-Lasky/Paramount; (5) William Wellman.

(1) *Victory*; (2) 1941; (3) USA; (4) Paramount; (5) John Cromwell.

Select Bibliography

This bibliography is divided into the following sections:
- A. Bibliographies
- B. Manuscripts
- C. Works by Conrad
- D. Biographies and letters
- E. Criticism: (i) books,
  (ii) essays and articles.

In recent years, publications on Conrad, especially in the area of criticism and interpretation, have been very numerous, and only a selection of the more important and interesting items is listed here. For discussions of specific works, see under the appropriate entries earlier in this volume.

A. BIBLIOGRAPHIES

T. J. Wise's bibliography of Conrad's writings (1920) does not include the productions of his final years. The standard sources are K. A. Lohf & E. P. Sheehy, *Joseph Conrad at Mid-Century: Editions and Studies 1895–1944* (Minneapolis, 1957), and T. G. Ehrsam, *A Bibliography of Joseph Conrad* (New Jersey, 1969), both of which include listings of criticism and other secondary works as well as Conrad's own writings. Another useful listing of Conrad criticism is by Maurice Beebe in a special Conrad number of *Modern Fiction Studies* (1955; updated in the same journal, 1964), and the journal *Conradiana* (from 1968) contains details of recent publications. A good short bibliography of primary and secondary material will be found in the *New Cambridge Bibliography of English Literature*, IV (1972), ed. I. R. Willison, cols 395–417. Theses on Conrad (1917–63) have been listed by E. A. & H. T. Bojarski (Lexington, 1964).

B. MANUSCRIPTS

For the early history of Conrad's manuscripts, see under Quinn in 'A Conrad Who's Who'. The largest collection is now in Philadelphia (A. S. W. Rosenbach

177

Foundation and Richard Gimpel Collection), and there are other significant collections at the British Library and at Harvard, Yale, Indiana, and the New York Public Library.

C. WORKS BY CONRAD

There have been numerous collected editions of Conrad's writings. The first of them was the 'Sun-dial' edition, a limited edition published in New York (1920–5); a version of it was issued by Heinemann of London (1921–7). Other editions include the 'Uniform' (1923–8) and the 'Kent' (1926). The texts of these editions are unsatisfactory and they do not include Conrad's plays, his unfinished novel *The Sisters*, or *The Nature of a Crime*, written jointly with Hueffer. Useful editions of three works have been included in the Norton Critical Edition series (New York): *Heart of Darkness*, ed. Robert Kimbrough (1963). *Lord Jim*, ed. Thomas C. Moser (1968), and *The Nigger of the 'Narcissus'*, ed. Robert Kimbrough (1979). Cambridge University Press have in preparation a complete critical edition of Conrad's works. For the original publication of individual works in serial and volume versions, see the appropriate entries earlier in this book.

Conrad has been translated into many languages. A complete edition of his works into Polish has been supervised by Zdzislaw Najder. For details of translations, see Ehrsam's bibliography (above).

The Garland Publishing Co. (New York) has issued concordances to most of Conrad's works in eighteen volumes.

There have been numerous anthologies of Conrad's work, of which one of the most substantial is *The Portable Conrad*, ed. M. D. Zabel (1947; rev. 1969).

D. BIOGRAPHIES AND LETTERS

Among early accounts of Conrad are two by close friends: Richard Curle's *The Last Twelve Years of Joseph Conrad* (1928), and Ford Madox Ford's *Joseph Conrad: A Personal Remembrance* (1924). Curle also published an essay, 'Conrad as I remember him', in the *Contemporary Review* (1959). Conrad's wife Jessie published two attractive books, *Joseph Conrad as I Knew him* (1926) and *Joseph Conrad and his Circle* (1935), and there are also books by Conrad's two sons: Borys Conrad's *My Father Joseph Conrad* (1970) and John Conrad's *Joseph Conrad: Times Remembered* (1981). For briefer accounts of Conrad by his contemporaries, see under Jacob Epstein, Frank Harris, Ottoline Morrell, Bertrand Russell and others in 'A Conrad Who's Who'.

Of more formal biographies, Gérard Jean-Aubry's *Joseph Conrad: Life and Letters*, 2 vols (1927) was for long a standard work but is now superseded by more recent biographies of which the most important are Jocelyn Baines' *Joseph Conrad: a Biography* (1960), Frederick R. Karl's *Joseph Conrad: the Three Lives* (New York, 1979), and Zdzislaw Najder's *Joseph Conrad: A Chronicle* (1983) – this last supplemented by the same author's *Conrad under Familial Eyes* (1983). Other works include Jerry Allen, *The Sea Years of Joseph Conrad* (New York, 1965); B. C. Meyer, *Joseph Conrad: A Psychoanalytic Biography* (Princeton, 1967); and Gustav Morf, *The Polish Heritage of Joseph Conrad* (1930) and *The Polish Shades and Ghosts of Joseph Conrad* (the titles of these four books all indicate their distinctive emphasis or bias). Norman Sherry's *Conrad's Eastern World* (1966) and *Conrad's Western World* (1971) contain much detailed biographical information.

From his early years, when he wrote in Polish or French, to the end of his life, Conrad was a prolific and energetic correspondent, and over 3500 of his letters have survived. They have been described as his 'true autobiography' and contain a great deal of biographical interest. There have been a number of collections of Conrad's letters to various individuals: to his wife (1927), to Richard Curle (1928), to Marguerite Poradowska (1940, translated from French), to the publishers William Blackwood and David Meldrum (1958), and to Cunninghame Graham (1969), among others. Recently (1983) the opening volume has appeared in a projected eight-volume *Collected Letters of Joseph Conrad*, which will clearly become the standard edition. Under the general editorship of Frederick R. Karl, it will contain all the surviving letters – over 3500 in all, of which some 1500 have not been previously published. This will obviously represent an important advance in our knowledge of Conrad; the first volume, covering the years 1861–97, is usefully annotated and includes maps and illustrations.

E. CRITICISM

(i) Books

A very useful collection of early criticism of Conrad (mainly reviews of individual works as they appeared) is *Conrad: the Critical Heritage*, ed. Norman Sherry (1973). The first book to be devoted to Conrad was Richard Curle's *Joseph Conrad: a Study* (1914). Other important earlier studies (to 1960) are:

M. C. Bradbrook, *Joseph Conrad: Poland's English Genius* (Cambridge, 1941).
Edward Crankshaw, *Joseph Conrad: Some Aspects of the Art of the Novel* (1936).
Adam Gillon, *The Eternal Solitary: a Study of Joseph Conrad* (New York, 1960).
J. D. Gordan, *Joseph Conrad: the Making of a Novelist* (Cambridge, Mass., 1940).
Albert J. Guerard, *Conrad the Novelist* (Cambridge, Mass., 1958).
Douglas Hewitt, *Conrad: A Reassessment* (Cambridge, 1952; rev. edns, 1969, 1975).
Frederick R. Karl, *A Reader's Guide to Joseph Conrad* (New York, 1960; rev. edn, 1969).
F. R. Leavis, *The Great Tradition* (1948).
R. L. Megroz, *Joseph Conrad's Mind and Method* (1931).
Thomas Moser, *Joseph Conrad: Achievement and Decline* (Cambridge, Mass., 1957).
E. H. Visiak, *The Mirror of Conrad* (1955).
Paul Wiley, *Conrad's Measure of Man* (Madison, 1954).

Of the numerous studies that have appeared in the past twenty-five years, the most important is probably Ian Watt's *Conrad in the Nineteenth Century* (1980), the first instalment of an extended study. Other notable accounts include:

Jeffrey Berman, *Joseph Conrad: Writing as Rescue* (New York, 1977).
Paul Bruss, *Conrad's Early Sea Fiction* (Lewisburg, 1979).
C. B. Cox, *Joseph Conrad: the Modern Imagination* (1974).
Andrew Davies, *Conrad's War* (1978).
Avrom Fleishman, *Conrad's Politics* (Baltimore, 1967).
Bell Gale, *Conrad and the Romantic Hero* (New Haven, 1962).
R. A. Gekoski, *Conrad: the Moral World of the Novelist* (1978).
Lawrence Graver, *Conrad's Short Fiction* (Berkeley, 1969).
Eloise Knapp Hay, *The Political Novels of Joseph Conrad* (Chicago, 1963).
John A. Palmer, *Joseph Conrad's Fiction: a Study in Literary Growth* (Ithaca, 1968).
E. W. Said, *Conrad and the Fiction of Autobiography* (Cambridge, Mass., 1966).
Daniel R. Schwarz, *'Almayer's Folly' to 'Under Western Eyes'* (1980).
Daniel R. Schwarz, *Conrad: the Later Fiction* (1982).
Werner Senn, *Conrad's Narrative Voice: Stylistic Aspects of his Fiction* (Bern, 1980).
J. I. M. Stewart, *Joseph Conrad* (1968).
David Thornburn, *Conrad's Romanticism* (New Haven, 1974).

(ii) Essays and Articles

Articles in periodicals and scholarly journals on Conrad are too numerous for even a partial listing to be attempted here; reference may be made to the bibliographies mentioned above and to the various annual bibliographies such as *The Year's Work in English Studies*. There have been various symposia devoted to Conrad, including an issue of the *London Magazine* (1957); *The Art of Conrad: a Critical Symposium*, ed. R. W. Stallman (East Lansing, 1960); *Joseph Conrad: Centennial Essays*, ed. L. Krzyzanowski (New York, 1960); and *Joseph Conrad: a Commemoration*, ed. Norman Sherry (1976). Among other collections of shorter pieces, there is a volume on Conrad in the 'Twentieth Century Views' series, ed. Marvin Mudrick (Englewood Cliffs, 1966), and two volumes in the 'Casebook Series' – one on *The Secret Agent*, ed. Ian Watt (1973), and one on *Heart of Darkness*, *Nostromo* and *Under Western Eyes*, ed. C. B. Cox (1981).

Other essays and chapters on Conrad will be found in the following:

Walter Allen, *Six Great Novelists* (1955).
Douglas Brown, 'From *Heart of Darkness* to *Nostromo*: an Approach to Conrad', in *Pelican Guide to English Literature, VII: The Modern Age*, ed. Boris Ford (Harmondsworth, 1961).
David Daiches, *The Novel and the Modern World* (Chicago, 1939; rev. edn, 1960).
E. M. Forster, *Abinger Harvest* (1936).
Graham Hough, *Image and Experience* (1960).
G. D. Killam, *Africa in English Fiction* (1968).
J. Hillis Miller, *Poets of Reality* (1965).
V. S. Pritchett, *The Living Novel* (1946); *The Tale Bearers* (1980).
J. I. M. Stewart, *Eight Modern Writers* (Oxford, 1963).
Raymond Williams, *The English Novel from Dickens to Lawrence* (1970).
Virginia Woolf, *The Common Reader* (1924); *The Captain's Death Bed* (1950).
M. D. Zabel, *Craft and Character in Modern Fiction* (New York, 1957).

Mention may also be made of some of the numerous studies that compare Conrad with – or trace the influence of, or his influence upon – other writers. He has been compared with Dickens by F. R. Karl (*Notes & Queries*, 1957), J. H. Walton (*Nineteenth Century Fiction*, 1968), and Norman Page (*Conradiana*, 1973); with T. S. Eliot by R. L. Morris (*Modern Language Notes*, 1950) and D. J. McConnell (*Texas Studies in Language & Literature*, 1962); with Ford Madox Ford by Samuel Hynes (*Sewanee Review*, 1965) and Hugh Kenner (*Gnomon*, 1958); with Thomas Hardy by R. G. Lillard (*Publications of the Modern Language Association*, 1935) and K. W. Hunt (*English Journal*, 1960); with Ernest Hemingway by W. B. Bache (*Modern Language Notes*, 1957); with Henry James by E. K. Brown (*Yale Review*, 1945) and in Elsa Nettels' *James and Conrad* (Athens, Georgia, 1977); with Kipling by John A. McClure in his *Kipling and Conrad* (Cambridge, Mass., 1981); with D. H. Lawrence by K. K. Ruthven (*Critical Quarterly*, 1968); with Thomas Mann by J. B. Kaye (*Comparative Literature*, 1957); with Maupassant by G. J. Worth (*Journal of English and Germanic Philology*, 1955) and P. Kirschner (*Review of English Studies*, 1965, 1966); with Melville by J. D. Green (*Modern Fiction Studies*, 1962); with Shakespeare by A. Sherbo (*Notes & Queries*, 1953) and in Adam Gillon's *Conrad and Shakespeare* (New York, 1976); with Turgenev by J. C. Maxwell (*Notes & Queries*, 1963); with Robert Penn Warren by S. L. Gross (*Twentieth Century Literature*, 1957); and with Zola by M. Chaikin (*Studies in Philology*, 1955).

Index

182